TROOPER

Robert S. Prout

ISBN 978-1-941142-73-8

Disclaimer

This is a work of fiction. Names, characters, businesses, agencies, places, events and incidents are either the products of the author's imagination or used in a fictitious manner. Any resemblance to actual persons, living or dead, or actual events is purely coincidental.

Cover Design by Debbie O'Byrne

Publishing and Design by JETLAUNCH Strategic Publishing
www.jetlaunch.net

TABLE OF CONTENTS

ABOUT THE AUTHOR

Robert Prout worked as a state highway patrolman, law-enforcement trainer, program developer, consultant, and professor. He holds a B.A. degree from Muskingum College, a LL.B. degree from LaSalle Extension University, a M.Ed. degree from Ohio University, and a Ph.D. degree from The Ohio State University.

This book is dedicated to my mentor, Ralph Lucas.

TO THE READER

When I began to think about writing a story about a rookie state trooper and the relationships that matured him, I read my journal that I started when I entered the highway patrol academy.

While you may disagree with how I present some situations and characters, please know they are a composite of experiences and individuals I've known. This is a story about the lives of ordinary people that is brought to life from my journal and my mind.

*A thousand words leave not the same deep
impression as does a single deed.*

Henrik Ibsen (1828 to 1906)

1

THE BOY

ON A JANUARY DAY IN 1965, Professor Victoria Whitcombe sat behind her office desk in Eaton Hall. Across from her sat one of the most promising of students, but she was going to lose him, the college was going to lose him, and she didn't know why.

"What's going on with you, Bill? It's all over campus you're quitting basketball . . . quitting college . . . going to—I can hardly believe what I've heard—a police academy!"

The handsome young man nodded, and his enthusiasm for his decision made him smile. "Yes, yes. After spring semester, Professor Whitcombe."

"I don't understand. You're throwing away your basketball scholarship . . . your college education . . . to be a *cop*! Really?"

"Not a cop," Bill Brand said. "A *State Trooper*, Professor Whitcombe." He seemed to swell as he said this.

Professor Whitcombe had seen students drop out of college. Most left without a word. What was different about this student was his conviction. She had geared herself to change his mind and keep this talented young man in college, but, in the face of his joyful determination, she deflated. "The academy starts when?"

"Monday after finals week."

She sighed. "Any chance I can talk you out of this?" she said, knowing she probably couldn't.

"Why would you want to, Professor Whitcombe?"

Why indeed. Still Professor Whitcombe found herself voicing the arguments she often used when she had this talk with students soon to leave school. "Don't be a quitter, Bill. Quitting's addictive. It's habit forming. Quitting's a bad personality trait."

Instead of shame, instead of a rendition of how expensive college was, she saw this last-ditch argument slide off this student.

Professor Victoria Whitcombe unconsciously turned sideways in her chair. She leaned back and put her heel on the second shelf of her bookcase. She just didn't know what to make of Bill. Her red skirt draped an inch below her knee.

"You'll be in my one o'clock Psychology 201 Section One session today . . . first class?"

He nodded, but he didn't lift his eyes from her leg. She blushed, realizing where his eyes had fixed.

She put her legs under her desk. She nodded. "I'm sorry, Bill. I hate to see you leave, but I see you're determined to do so. Good luck to you."

Bill thanked her and got up. As he turned and walked from her office, she thought, *Nice butt.* When Bill had gone, she rolled her eyes at herself. *Dear God in heaven, what's wrong with me? What made me show him my leg? What made me notice his butt? He's a twenty-year-old kid! Just a boy!*

* * *

At *precisely* one o'clock, Professor Victoria Whitcombe entered her classroom and closed the Psychology 201 door. She scanned the full room. There were no empty seats.

Professor Whitcombe looked the class over and gave the class her typical opening lines, "We breathe like animals. We eat like animals. We drink like animals. We defecate like animals. We urinate like animals. We fornicate like animals. Everyone in this room, and that includes me, *is an animal.* Get used to the fact that we're bipedal primates. You and I are members of a single species within the clade of mammals, a clade being just a branch on the tree of life. You and I got our start in Ethiopia about 200,000 years ago. That's about 10,000 breeding cycles. Seems like a long time ago, but that's too short of a time for our brains to evolve and catch up to today's complex world."

She said this as she walked to the front of the room. There she put her notes on the podium. She looked over the students for a dramatic moment.

"Everyone ... and that also includes me ... has mental issues. How can we not? For some of us, these issues take the form of full-blown mental illness. For others," she said with a shrug, "they're just a collection of traits."

Mild laughter followed, and she smiled.

"Welcome to Psychology 201, Section 1. I'm Professor Victoria Whitcombe. Do check to see you're in the right place."

Another round of laughter, a little more inclusive this time.

"Even if you are in the class you signed up for, you might want to reconsider. If you can't handle that we're animals, if you can't handle that we aren't special, if you can't handle that we all have mental traits or illnesses, I suggest you drop Section One and take Section Two from Professor Clausen. His class meets in Room 333 at two o'clock. I checked before I came to class ... seats are available."

She did this at the course beginning each semester. Sometimes students did get up and leave, slinking off in embarrassment, but she was pleased that no one got up this time.

"Any questions?" asked Professor Whitcombe.

"What about God?" a girl asked.

"I don't understand your question. What do you mean?"

"God created us in his image. God is above the animals. So are we. I've been called a lot of things in my life, Professor Whitcombe, but *I have never been called an animal!* I don't even know what you mean."

"How do you define God?" asked Professor Whitcombe, not in the least perturbed.

The girl blinked. "God's the Supreme Being. He knows everything. We *are* his special creation," said the girl.

Brand raised his hand.

"Yes, Bill."

"It'd help us understand your position better, Professor Whitcombe, if you would give us your definition of God."

She studied Brand a moment. She looked at the class. "My definition of God. Okay. For me God is 'order in the universe.'"

"I don't understand what you mean," said the girl.

For a moment Professor Whitcombe looked up at the ceiling as if the explanation were written in the worn acoustic tiles.

"Order in the universe means nothing truly dies. It means everything is simply transformed. Nothing is wasted," said Professor Whitcombe. "Not ever."

Another student asked, "Professor Whitcombe, do you believe in God?"

"I do," she said and left it at that. She waited a long moment, then said, "Okay, no more questions? I'll let you out early today ... *but only today* ... to give you time to consider just in case you really want to change to Dr. Clausen's section. But before I release you, I want to expand on one thing I told you. I said we all have mental issues. In past years, psychology had this all-or-nothing perspective. A person was either mentally ill, or he or she wasn't. This view has changed. We now see things differently. We now see mental illness and mental wellness as part of the same continuum. Yes, there are people who have obsessive-compulsive disorders, and others have obsessive-compulsive traits. Yes, some of us get obsessed from time to time, but that doesn't mean we're clinically obsessed." She paused, wondering if she were obsessed.

"Some traits are good to have. Attention to detail is a personality trait. Ability to focus is a personality trait. We want our pilots, our doctors, dentists, plumbers, bus drivers to have high attention to detail. We want them focused. I hope you want your teachers to have high attention to detail, too ... to be focused."

She could see the girl who had started the questioning was listening intently, clearly looking for a handle to hold to in her class. She had seen this look before. This student would stay, thirsty to learn, even if some things jarred her long-held beliefs. Professor Whitcombe continued, "Yes, some people have social anxiety disorders, and others are just plain shy. The first might need lots of help and some medication. The second . . . well, a shy person is just a shy person. Chances are she or he was born that way. Shyness is a trait. It's not a disorder."

Laughter.

"Yes, most of us get depressed from time to time, but most of the time, we're happy. We're not depressed in the clinical sense.

"There, I've said what I wanted to say. If you change sections, I don't want you believing I said we're all mentally ill. Whether you leave or stay, I want you to remember brain health is on a continuum ranging from normal personality traits at one end of the spectrum to full-blown mental illnesses on the other end. Each of us is somewhere on the continuum at different times in our lives, and, sometimes, our position on that spectrum changes.

"Have compassion toward others because of this: The Department of Health said one quarter of the population has some psychiatric illness and half of us risk developing one. Common ones are anxiety, substance abuse, narcissism, obsessive-compulsive disorder, and depression. I'm sure you know people who are mentally ill even though you and they may not know it. Always remember: they didn't ask for their pathologies."

As a form of dismissal, she stepped back from her podium, adding, "We'll begin an intellectual ride like you've never before taken come one o'clock Wednesday. That is, if you've got the guts to come back! Class dismissed."

*   *   *

That semester, like those before it, played out pretty much as Professor Victoria Whitcombe expected. After she had corrected Bill Brand's final examination, she wrote on his paper: "*Course grade B+. Bill, please call me, 340-7751, just as soon as you finish your cop training. Victoria.*"

*   *   *

The man with whom Victoria Whitcombe had had a long-term relationship was a professor. She knew other professors like him, men who believed they were entitled, who believed they deserved their professorships. She'd seen so many men who basked in the words *professor* and *doctor*. She wondered what kind of men they had been before they became professors.

She wondered if they had ever been take-charge men, if getting a doctorate degree and working at the university had weakened them. She wondered why these men talked so much, but said so little, why they hid in the passive voice and used so many adverbs. They used big words when smaller words worked better, started their classes late and ended them early. They lacked common sense. She wondered most why these men didn't have a clue how the real world worked.

Most good professors did research in the real world *or* had real jobs in the real world before they became college professors.

Victoria accepted that academia wasn't the real world. Professors lived in ivory towers protected by tenure—jobs for life. Handsome retirement checks awaited them. The university was their patron saint.

* * *

Early Saturday morning, Victoria grabbed two brown grocery bags and the classified section of the newspaper. She had circled three garage-sale ads that listed books. With her mission laid out, she drove from the university. But Professor Victoria Whitcombe wasn't looking for academic books. She was looking for books to add to a collection she kept in her bedroom closet.

* * *

Hours later, the fruits of her garage-sale purchases hidden in the brown grocery bags, Victoria knelt in her open closet and neatly placed her new books beside the collection already in her closet in the order she would read them. Though the shelves of her living room and bedroom were filled with hardcover classics—books any professor would be proud to own, her back closet wall was stacked with her secret stash of paperback romance novels. *Am I obsessed* she wondered. This and coming weekends she would read of new loves and each romantic hero would be *her* hero, *her* man.

Finished with her stacking, Victoria leaned back on her heels and wondered if the note she wrote on Brand's final examination paper would be enough to get him to call.

*   *   *

At that moment, however, Bill Brand was not thinking of Victoria in any part. Instead, he stood in a line with other young men, facing a tall, broad-shouldered man with a severe military crew cut. The man faced the young men, looking anything but cheerful.

"Gentlemen, my name's Trooper Bice. I'm your physical training instructor. A significant part of any instruction in physical training is to know the proper method of making your bed . . . yes, gentlemen, *b-e-d.*"

Bill didn't quite know what this Trooper Bice meant by that, but, like the other men, he didn't ask, just waited.

"Gentlemen," Bice continued, "when I get through with you, you *will* love your bed. Each week, you'll be issued two clean sheets and one clean pillowcase."

They stood in a barracks, and Trooper Bice motioned them to gather around the metal frame of a bed with a naked mattress.

The thirty-eight cadets shuffled in a circle around the bed.

"Gentlemen, tuck the pillow under your chin. Place your thumbs inside the pillowcase. Be sure to have the pillowcase's seam under your right thumb. Spread the opening of the pillowcase. Work the pillowcase over the pillow."

The pillow was quickly encased by its cover.

Brand thought this pedantic, and he figured the rest of the new recruits did as well, but Trooper Bice looked formidable enough that he wasn't about to make mention of this.

"Gentlemen, fit the sheet over the mattress exactly even with the top edge of the mattress. Fold the bottom end of the sheet tightly under the foot and the other end tightly under the head of the mattress. Now, gentlemen, the sides of the sheet are folded tightly under the mattress. Watch. Tuck each side of the sheet at the top and bottom of the mattress precisely at forty-five-degree angles. Be sure there are no wrinkles. Gentlemen, the second sheet and blanket are secured exactly the same as the first sheet."

The trooper meticulously demonstrated the process.

"Gentlemen, the next step is to fold the uppermost sheet at the head of the bunk over this top blanket and secure both sides under the mattress. Be sure to have only a six-inch fold of sheet . . . and be sure there are absolutely no wrinkles."

Trooper Bice pulled a six-inch ruler from his pocket.

"Gentlemen, note the fold is neither five-and-three-quarters inches, nor is it six-and-one-quarter inches. The fold is exactly six inches. I want you to be precise."

In silence the young recruits watched as Trooper Bice measured the exposed sheet at each edge of the mattress and in the middle of the bed. Though he had made the fold without the rule to guide him, each time he placed the rule on the sheet, it measured exactly six inches.

"Take the pillow, gentlemen, and place the loose edges of the pillowcase under the pillow. Center the pillow at the head of the bunk. Gentlemen, smooth out every wrinkle. I better not see even one wrinkle. Are there questions?"

No cadet spoke. *Who would dare?* thought Brand.

Trooper Bice straightened and pointed to another trooper standing next to a cart loaded with sheets and blankets. "Fine. Sign out two sheets, one pillowcase, and one blanket. Proceed to your assigned sleeping area and make your bed. Report to the exercise field in thirty minutes for some light calisthenics. And, just so you understand, thirty minutes is not thirty minutes and one second. Report in proper gear for physical training."

The cadets formed a line and procured their bedding. Then they made their beds. Brand found himself making his bed over and over before he felt he had duplicated the demonstrated technique Trooper Bice had showed them. Most of the rest of the recruits did the same. Unbelievably, the effort of making the bed had left Brand and others with a scant five minutes to dress and dash out to the field. He arrived with a minute to spare.

At exactly thirty minutes from the time he had left them to make their beds, Trooper Bice appeared on the training field. All cadets were present, though a few were sweating and panting.

"I'm sure all of you carefully screened individuals followed the correspondence you received, and you're in top physical shape. To demonstrate this to me, line up in two rows with the tallest men in front. According to decreasing height, extend the rows. We'll jog only two miles to get loosened up for calisthenics. Keep a distance of three feet between each man. That's one yard, gentlemen."

The jogging began. While he jogged, Brand thought of how the next fourteen weeks might go. He had followed the exercise requirements he'd received. Worked hard at it, too, though they had not been much different from his basketball exercises. He knew he could easily handle the jogging. Basketball had prepared him well.

As he jogged, trying to pace himself so the man behind him could maintain that one-yard gap between them, Brand thought about his mother and father. He thought about how they had pushed him to excel in basketball, so he could get a college scholarship and not live a laborer's life like they had. He thought about how sad his mother and he had been at his father's funeral six months earlier.

He thought, too, of Mandy, of how she wanted him to stay in college. Like most everyone else, she hadn't understood how he could give up his studies and basketball. He thought of her body, of how they had both agreed they were too young to be in an exclusive relationship. Some college athletes paired up with coeds, not only for sex, but also for companionship and to get help with their studies. He thought about his upcoming weekend leaves from the academy and his promise they would spend their Friday nights and Saturday mornings in her apartment.

The two miles breezed by. Brand was lean and tall, his long legs made for running. He felt he could run forever.

Brand, being tall, had led one line, and Cadet Shaw led the other. Shaw and Brand then lined up for calisthenics. Only then did Brand see that many cadets had not kept pace. He saw Shaw look at the broken lines. Were they responsible for the men behind them? Gaps, some nearly ten yards yawned where cadets had been unable to keep up, and the men behind them had been forced to slow their pace. In his own line several such ragged spacing pointed out which men had not maintained the exercise guidelines.

The cadets assembled on the field. Trooper Bice said nothing about those who had not kept pace. They were told to lie down on the grass. The night was cool. The ground was damp.

"Gentlemen, the patrol has its own special sit-up. Place your right hand under your left armpit. Place your left hand under your right armpit. Keep your legs slightly bent and together. At the command of 'one,' rise to a forty-five-degree position and hold it. At 'two' rise to the ninety-degree position. Command 'three' is back to the forty-five-degree position, and 'four' is back to prone. Begin. One, two, three, four. Again. One, two, three, four. Again."

Five minutes passed. Brand could hear men grunting with effort. The cadets were fading under the continuous commands.

"One!"

Many of the cadets automatically continued to the number two position. They jerked back to the forty-five-degree position.

They waited for Bice to say, "Two."

Command "two" didn't come. They strained to hold the forty-five-degree position. Even Brand began to find this hard.

A cadet in the front row collapsed backwards, gasping.

"Your name, cadet?" asked Trooper Bice.

The cadet didn't answer.

Trooper Bice knelt and screamed in the face of the cadet who had collapsed backwards. "Your name, cadet?"

"Gillis. My name is Gillis."

"Gillis," said Bice, nodding almost thoughtfully. "So you're that pimply-assed deputy sheriff who wanted to join a man's outfit. Did ya get the workout instructions three months ago?"

"Yeah."

"Yeah? What kind of a word is that?"

Gillis swallowed, trying hard to catch his breath. He said, "Yes."

"Yes what?"

Brand expected Gillis to reply, "Yes, sir."

Gillis said nothing. He glared up at Trooper Bice, clambered to his feet and walked to the barracks.

The cadets couldn't hold position "one" any longer, regardless of their desire to be state troopers. They were moaning.

Bice, watching Gillis, said, "Two, three, four," and the cadets gratefully lay panting.

Calisthenics continued with forty push-ups. Then Bice said, "Two laps around the field, gentlemen."

The cadets, exhausted to the point of not caring, rose and began the circuit of the field. As Brand came around for the second pass, he saw Gillis, his suitcase in hand, walk to the parking lot.

The first cadet had quit.

As Brand ran, he thought of Professor Whitcombe's words, "Don't be a quitter, Bill." He thought of her leg and her red skirt.

He wondered why she'd given him her private phone number. He wondered why she wanted him to call her. He hardly remembered when he had finished the two circuits of the field and gone with the rest back to the barracks, then supper, then bed.

*   *   *

At half-past five in the morning, a whistle sounded, jarring Brand out of deep sleep. A voice followed: "Be on the field at six o'clock in exercise gear and in the proper formation. Your sleeping area is to be secured before you report."

Trooper Bice had blown the whistle and gave them their orders. Another trooper met them at exactly six o'clock. He was an older trooper.

"Gentlemen, I'm Captain Jorden, one of your instructors. From this point forward you'll stand at attention when a trooper approaches you. You'll remain at attention until the command 'At Ease' is given. Is that clear?" Without waiting for any confirmation of that, he said, "Now, follow me."

The cadets, in formation, followed Captain Jorden around the track. After the second lap, the captain stepped aside. He ordered the cadets to break rank and to run at top speed for two additional laps. Brand smiled. He loved to run. He increased his lead with almost every stride of his long legs. He finished first.

Their early exercise period finished, they jogged to the showers. A cadet said to Brand, "Where in hell's the fire? Why'd you run so fast? Whatcha tryin' to do, make the rest of us look bad?"

Brand said, "No . . . I was just following the captain's orders. He ordered to run at top speed. I did." Shaw and

Brand had had an eighteen-yard lead over the cadets at the rear plus a lead on everyone else. Having long legs helped. But it called to mind Professor Whitcombe saying in class not to take pride in your abilities because everyone was just an actor playing the part written from our genes and our environments.

The cadets showered and dressed in their cadet uniforms.

At 7:15 a.m., Trooper Bice appeared in the barracks. The cadets stood at attention.

"Gentlemen, just like there's a right way to make a bed, it shouldn't surprise you that there's a proper method of entering the dining room. Line up on each side of the hallway as if you're reporting for physical training, tallest in front. The first cadet who sees a trooper approaching is to yell 'Ten-hut!' Understand?"

No one said anything, but remained rigidly at attention.

"At ease, gentlemen. Line up for breakfast. When you hear the whistle, march to the dining area. Remain at attention behind your chair. When you hear the command, 'Seats,' you sit. Sit erectly. Talk limitedly. Eat your meal, then leave the dining area when finished. You're allotted fifteen minutes to eat. Report to your first class at eight o'clock."

* * *

"Ten-hut," said a trooper near the classroom door.

The cadets stood and snapped to attention. A major entered. He walked to the front of the classroom.

"Seats," said the trooper.

In unison, the cadets sat. They sat erectly.

"Gentlemen, my name is Major Armstrong. I'm commandant of the State Patrol Academy. I welcome the sixty-seventh academy class. Those of you still with us fourteen weeks from now, will have had excellent instruction that will have prepared you to enter active duty. Remember, I said you'll have had excellent instruction that *will have prepared you* to enter active duty. For those of you who successfully complete these fourteen weeks of training, I want you to be proud of what you've accomplished, but, also, I want you to be humble because I want you to know how little you'll know. I want you to be hard on yourselves throughout your career because I want you to continue to learn and to improve. You'll never have all the answers. You'll never be perfect. You *will* make mistakes. Your commissioning certificate is a license to learn. A good trooper loves learning.

"After you've been a trooper for a few years comes a dangerous time. When a trooper does his job day after day, it becomes commonplace. But becoming lackadaisical and complacent will get you injured or killed. There are other risks. You'll see so much of the tragic and seamy side of life that your spirit, if you let it, will get injured or killed, too. Don't let it.

"I joined the Highway Patrol thirty years ago. I want to share with you something my instructor said to my cadet class. It served me well these thirty years. It's an excellent piece of advice.

"I followed it. He said we should make a *Thoughts-for-Living* list. We should carry that list in our pocket every day of our lives and to tell our loved ones to make sure our list is in our pocket when we are in our coffins. He said when we're having a rough day to take out our list and read it. I've added to and taken from my list throughout these many years. I'm not going to give you a copy of my list because some of what is on my list doesn't yet apply to you, and may never apply. You'll need to learn for yourselves what to put on your list, but I've chosen four thoughts from my list for you to consider using when you start your list. These thoughts may help you survive your fourteen weeks of training. The sergeant will give each of you a copy of those four thoughts at the end of this class. They are: *1. People are who they are; therefore, acknowledge their reasons that give them peace of mind. If they change, it's usually on their own initiative, independent of, and often resistant to, pressure or expectations from me. 2. The art of being wise is the art of knowing what to overlook. 3. Don't do anything with the expectation of being appreciated. 4. Be calm. Some things are up to me, and some things are not up to me.* These thoughts come from the *Enchiridion*. The *Enchiridion* is a handbook that instructs the reader how to live wisely.

I recommend you study the *Enchiridion* after you're commissioned.

"That is all."

* * *

Daily different instructors spoke of boxing week and how that week would be the downfall for all but the most resilient cadets. Of the original thirty-eight cadets who began the course, thirty-four men remained at the beginning of the seventh week.

"Next week, gentlemen, I'm sure you're all aware is boxing week. It's imperative you continue to demonstrate determination during this period. To continue your preparation for next week, we have a seven-mile, cross-country run this afternoon. You're to report in proper gear at two o'clock."

The run began. Trooper Bice set the pace. Slow. The run took the cadets through fields, over fences and hills. Brand stayed in the middle to avoid comments from the other cadets that he was showing off or running too fast.

* * *

Thirty-two cadets remained for boxing week. The instructors said nothing of the missing men.

"Shaw and Brand, put on your headgear and gloves," said Trooper Bice.

Brand thought he shouldn't be too aggressive, to fight only as if it were his duty to fight. He wouldn't call attention to himself.

The highway-patrol superintendent and command staff had come to the academy for boxing week. They sat in the front row. Brand wondered if they expected each cadet to be aggressive, but, surely, he wasn't meant to injure his boxing opponent. He considered his options. Shaw was twenty-eight. Brand was twenty. Shaw was taller and more muscular. Shaw had never mentioned he'd boxed for a Marine Corps boxing team. The bell sounded.

Keep my left up ... keep my left up, Brand repeated silently while he took continuous blows to his body. Then Shaw changed tactics and hit him with a powerful right hook.

When Brand woke, all he remembered was Shaw's glove two feet from the left side of his face.

"Cadet Brand, ya got fifteen minutes to recover, then back in the ring, this time with Rodgers," said Trooper Bice.

Brand now realized what was expected of him. He *must* be aggressive. He thought, *I can't be hurt worse than getting knocked out again.*

While he was waiting for the fifteen minutes to pass, he wondered what the command staff wanted to see. He wondered why the command staff made the long drive to watch boxing and not show up for other phases of training. He wondered if a future trooper would attempt to hurt another future trooper, what he'd do to the public he'd taken an oath to protect and to serve. He wondered if the purpose of boxing week was to weed-out cadets too aggressive for the job or to demonstrate that a cadet had resilience . . . that he wasn't a quitter.

I quit college. I quit basketball, Brand thought, then firmed his jaw. *Even if I'm beaten to a pulp, I won't quit!* He thought of Professor's Whitcombe's statement— "Don't be a quitter, Bill."

Rodgers was shorter but more muscular than Brand. Brand threw several jabs at him. He didn't want to hurt him. Rodgers pursued Brand around the ring.

Trooper Bice's whistle blew. "Novak, you're next. You're fightin' Brand!"

Trooper Bice walked up to Brand and whispered harshly in his ear, "You either try to knock his head off, or I'll personally see that you never graduate! You be aggressive. Hit! Hit! Hit!"

The bell rang. Novak swung wildly, his head down. Brand stepped left, mustered all his strength, and hit Novak in the face with an upper-cut. Novak was on his back unconscious, bleeding. Brand approached Novak to help him.

"Get back, Brand," commanded Trooper Bice.

Brand had broken Novak's nose. Brand and Shaw weren't ordered to fight again, and Brand wondered if this was their reward for showing aggression.

*   *   *

"Gentlemen, line up opposite men your own size. We're goin' to begin your training in defensive tactics by a demonstration of breaking the grasp of a person choking you. Line one, you're doing the choking. Line two, you're the troopers going to get choked. But before you can break a choke hold, you gotta know what it's like being choked. Line one will choke line two on command. Choke as hard as you can. Release your grip immediately when you hear the whistle. But I want you to choke your opponent in a specific way. Use the sides of your hands. Don't apply pressure with your thumbs. You'll injure the larynx.

"This is important. Line two, you will not resist. You'll keep your hands at your sides and keep your chins up while your being choked," commanded Trooper Bice.

Brand had to admit he was nervous as this exercise was explained. He had to let Shaw choke him. Could he do that?

"Choke!"

Shaw was powerful. With the insides of his hands he pressed hard against the sides of Brand's neck. Brand felt no pain. Oddly, he felt only the pressure from Shaw's hands. He'd expected to be gasping for air, but Shaw had put no pressure on his windpipe. At the five-second mark he no longer heard the rest of the cadets. He never heard the whistle. He just awoke to find himself on the ground blinking up at Shaw. He quickly stood and got back in line two, acting as if nothing had happened. It was as if he had awakened from a nap. He looked around. Most of line two was on the ground, but only Cadet Arnold was thrashing, a reaction that reminded Brand of the times his mother chopped off chicken heads and the headless birds flopped around. Arnold stopped thrashing, woke up and got to his feet. Like Brand, he acted as if nothing had happened.

Then the roles were reversed and Brand had his hands on Shaw's neck. He was amazed how quickly Shaw collapsed.

When the men again stood in two lines facing each other Bice said, "Line two, just before the hands of the cadets in line one reach your necks, tuck your chins as closely to your necks as you can. Line one, choke as hard as you can, but, again, don't put pressure on the larynx. Release your grip immediately when you hear the whistle. Choke!"

Trooper Bice blew the whistle at six seconds. The choking this time had affected no one in line two.

After the roles were again reversed, Trooper Bice said, "Gentlemen, you'll learn two methods of breaking choke holds. One method is used to incapacitate your adversary. The other method is used to kill your adversary if it's necessary to use deadly force," said Trooper Bice.

The instructor demonstrated the moves. The cadets practiced them. They learned defensive tactics. They could disarm adversaries and apply various holds to move individuals without injuring them. They learned how to disable a person without leaving a bruise. Firearms, criminal law, traffic law, accident investigation, report writing, first aid, pursuit driving, etiquette, procedures, rules, and regulations were taught.

The cadets learned the types of patrol stations throughout the state. Patrol posts were rated high, moderate, or low activity in relation to the amount of traffic and enforcement needed. The cadets who graduated with the highest scores would receive the coveted high-activity posts.

Finally it was over. All of it. Brand had stayed with the course all the way through and graduated. He had not quit.

*   *   *

"Sir, Trooper Brand reporting for duty, as ordered."

"You're early. It's noon. Your tour-of-duty doesn't start until four o'clock."

"I know, sir. I just wanted to be here."

"Ah, very good," said the lieutenant, smiling. "How was the traffic up here from General Headquarters?"

"Heavy, sir."

"Trooper Brand, your first name's Bill. Correct?"

"Correct, sir."

"Well, Bill, like I said, your tour of duty begins at four o'clock. You'll work the same shifts Trooper Lakes works. There are some forms you need to process. Get in uniform. Take any one of the three bunks in the barracks."

Brand noticed the leather holster, belt, and shoes of the lieutenant weren't spit shined like those of the academy troopers.

He walked to his truck for his uniforms and suitcase. He had been issued five shirts, two pairs of summer trousers, two pairs of winter trousers, a belt, summer and winter Stetsons, two jackets, a raincoat, a winter coat, two pairs of shoes, a handgun, a holster, a belt, handcuffs, buttons, a badge, a nameplate, a whistle, and a chain. It seemed like a lot of gear.

He took the far bunk, already noticing that the bunks weren't made to the military standard of the academy bunks. The folds weren't precisely six inches.

He wasn't to go on duty for four hours, but he was happy the lieutenant had told him to get into his uniform.

The lieutenant handed Brand the forms to read and sign. While completing them, a man cautiously opened the station's door.

"Me, my wife, and kids moved up here from Mississippi. I got a job. Yessir, I got a job over at the foundry. I gotta get new license plates, but the man down at the courthouse said I gotta get my car inspected. Sir, we ain't got much money, but I gotta get those plates," said the man.

The lieutenant came from his office to listen. The dispatcher, who wasn't a trooper, looked at the lieutenant. The lieutenant looked at Brand.

"Trooper Brand, you handle this title inspection," ordered the lieutenant. He turned and walked back to his office.

Brand looked at the apologetic man.

"Sir, may I see your Mississippi title certificate? Please understand the reason for this inspection is to limit the flow of stolen vehicles into the state. It's a procedure we do for all vehicles of new state residents."

"Yessir," said the man as he produced a much-folded title.

Brand looked at the old Ford. He knew the vehicle needed a safety inspection, but he also knew he only had authority from the lieutenant for a title check. He wondered if that had been on purpose or was an oversight.

"You see," continued Brand, "this is how it goes. Someone steals an automobile . . . let's say a late-model Cadillac. The car thief then searches around for an identical-modeled Cadillac. He'll pry loose and steal the serial-number tag and license plates and puts on a set of license plates that are from an old, inexpensive vehicle that isn't stolen. From the stolen Cadillac, he removes the correct serial-number tag and attaches the stolen one. He puts on the license plates from the Cadillac he took the serial-number tag and license plates. The car thief then figures he's got time to get the stolen Cadillac titled in another state before the owner of the identical-modeled Cadillac notices he has different license plates. In fact, some people don't know about the switch until they attempt to renew their tags or sell their car. The car thief types up a new title with the serial number from the identical-modeled Cadillac. He takes the stolen Cadillac to another state, files for and gets a clean title and the new state's license plates. Because the license plates and serial number aren't reported stolen, he gets a clear title to the stolen vehicle."

Brand gave this speech by rote, but he saw the man from Mississippi didn't understand. He just nodded and said, "Yessir, I see."

Brand looked at how the serial tag was attached, making sure it was done correctly. He verified that the serial-tag number matched the number on the Mississippi title. He signed the paper for the Bureau of Motor Vehicles. The man, now visibly relieved, slowly drove away from the patrol-post's parking lot.

"Serial tag in order?" asked the lieutenant.

"It was, sir."

"Why didn't ya do a safety inspection?"

"Would've, sir, if you'd told me to. They told us at the academy we weren't to do anything the first three months of our breaking-in period unless we're told to do it."

The lieutenant smiled. "Good thinkin', Trooper. By the way, you think he understood everything you said?"

"No, sir. Next time I won't talk so much."

"You're learnin', Trooper. Don't say more than you have to. And when you talk, be brief and to the point. Most times, you won't get yourself in trouble for something ya *don't* say."

Brand knew the vehicle would've failed the safety inspection. *Then what? The man couldn't have driven the car from the lot if it had been judged unsafe. If he had as little money as he'd said, how could he afford to get his car fixed? What about his wife and kids in the car? How would they get home?* That made sense. Then he had another thought. *But what if they're in an accident because the car was unsafe? What if someone else was injured or killed? A safety inspection may have prevented that.* He knew a case like this was never discussed at the academy. He knew he had a lot to learn.

Brand completed the forms and returned them to the lieutenant.

*   *   *

"Wanna go to lunch with us, Trooper?" asked the lieutenant.

"Sure do. Thank you, sir."

Brand quickly got in the back seat of the squad car. The lieutenant drove. The sergeant sat in the front seat.

While eating lunch the sergeant asked, "Tell us a little about ya, Bill." Bill wiped his mouth with his napkin. "Well, I had my twenty-first birthday yesterday."

"Whoa, you're only twenty-one! You've gotta be the youngest state trooper in the whole state. How'd you survive training? Troopers we get up here are older. You must've really impressed the academy staff to have them post you here."

"Don't know, sir."

"Okay, tell us more."

"Since grade school I wanted to be a state trooper. I played basketball in high school and got an opportunity to play college ball, so I took it. No one in my family ever went to college."

"So how come you aren't in college now?"

"Six months ago after basketball practice, I went to a state patrol recruiting presentation on campus. Next day I drove to the patrol post, filled out an application, and got accepted to the next academy class. It started right after the semester ended. Graduated from the academy Friday, and, well, here I am."

"What about your education? What about basketball?"

Brand nodded. "Education is important to me, but when I heard the trooper's presentation, just couldn't wait two more years to be a state trooper."

"Well stated, Trooper," said the lieutenant.

The sergeant nodded and said, "Yup."

The lieutenant, sergeant, and Brand each got separate checks for their meals. Brand looked at his. It had a line drawn just under the cost of the lunch. Under the line was the number "2." To the right of the line was an equal sign and then the amount for a half-priced lunch.

Brand looked at the other two checks and saw the same thing. He thought, *we're each charged half price!* At the academy, they told us to never take a meal at half price because it was the start of the slippery slope of becoming corrupt. The instructor said restaurants that give police officers half-priced meals and convenience stores that give officers free coffee did it for a reason. They liked squad cars parked outside because it was good for their businesses. People knew it was a safer place if police officers were inside. They also knew the food was good if the police ate there.

But Brand also remembered the instructor saying, "If you frequent those places, you're not providing equal protection to those restaurants and convenience stores that don't give half-priced meals and free coffee. You're accepting a bribe!"

Brand remembered the instructor ended his presentation with, "Troopers don't take welfare. Troopers treat everyone equally."

My god, thought Brand, *my first shift doesn't start until four, and I'm already being offered something I was told never to take, and right in front of my sergeant and post commander. Is this a set up? Could they be testing me to see if I'd take the half-priced meal? Or are they looking to see if I'm so straight-laced I'll call attention to stuff that doesn't measure up to academy standard. I'll be labeled a pain in the ass. That I won't go along to get along. Or am I just mountain climbing over a molehill? The safest bet for me is to do exactly what the lieutenant and the sergeant do.*

He followed the lieutenant and sergeant to the cash register. The lieutenant, the sergeant, and then Brand paid the half price to the cashier. But then the lieutenant and the sergeant walked back to the table. Brand followed. The two men put the change the cashier gave them on the table then took a dollar from their billfolds and put it on the table. Brand followed suit. He was enormously relieved, and he was learning.

2

THE MENTOR

USUAL SPOT?" ASKED TROOPER Ron Lakes. "Right. Highway 12 at Holiday Inn," said the dispatcher. Lakes checked with the lieutenant to verify that Brand had processed his papers. The lieutenant introduced Brand to Lakes, who was to be Brand's field-training instructor.

"Let's go, Bill," ordered Lakes.

Brand felt his command was more like a request and wasn't sure what they were doing or where they were going. He followed promptly, however. Brand got in the passenger's seat of patrol car 953 and fastened his seatbelt. Lakes's squad car was spotless.

He didn't ask Lakes what was happening because he didn't want to question his superior, but mostly he didn't want Lakes to know he didn't know.

Lakes fastened his seatbelt and eased car 953 into the rush hour traffic. Almost immediately they were traveling at high speed. Lakes put on his pursuit light.

He slowed almost to a stop at red lights and stop signs, but kept going and sounded his siren when he eased through intersections. Brand had no clue what was up.

"What we're on is a 'blood run,'" Lakes finally said.

Brand nodded as if he knew exactly what that meant.

The city-police car waited at the Holiday Inn.

"You get it," Lakes said. "Be sure to grip it under the cardboard box, so it doesn't drop out. Blood comes in a plastic bag packed in ice."

Brand jumped from the patrol car. He took the box from the city cop and gripped it carefully. As soon as he was seated and getting belted in, they were off again. At the interstate highway, Lakes pushed the Ford to over 120 miles per hour.

Brand had never been at these speeds, but he trusted that Lakes knew what he was doing and tried to relax and not let it bother him. At their destination, a small hospital in a nearby town, Troopers Lakes and Brand got out. Lakes locked the squad, while Brand continued to carry the blood. Lakes spoke to a nurse. He told her they had an emergency delivery of blood. She told Brand to put the box on the counter.

"Let's stay here in the waiting room a few minutes," said Lakes.

After five minutes Lakes got up, sauntered over to the room where they had left the blood and looked in. He walked back to Brand and said, "Let's go."

A short distance from the emergency room, Lakes telephoned the lieutenant. "Lieutenant, this is Ron.

Here's another one. Right, we're at Mercy Hospital. Blood hasn't moved from where we put it. Right, lieutenant."

Lakes asked Brand what he thought of the telephone conversation. "Seems like this wasn't such an emergency," said Brand.

"Sure appears that way. We drive at the edge of the envelope to get it to them, and they aren't even waiting for it. And this has happened several times. We think the hospital's using us for a delivery service. That's why I called the lieutenant. He'll find out what's up."

Brand nodded.

"Am I correct in thinking you've been advised of the procedure for your first six months?" asked Lakes.

"Right, sir."

"For the first three months, you'll do only what I tell you to do. For example, when I stop a vehicle, you'll get out and stay at the right rear of the stopped vehicle. Don't approach me unless I tell you. Is that clear?"

"Yes, sir."

A brown dog trotted into the intersection where they'd stopped for a red light. A car hit the dog.

Lakes and Brand watched the dog slide and tumble thirty feet into the intersection. The dog then sat, breathed deeply, whined, and seemed to be looking but not seeing.

Lakes flipped on the pursuit light and drove to the intersection. Brand walked slightly behind Lakes to the dog.

The dog's right hind leg was in a grotesque position. A small, white, jagged-edged bone protruded two inches beyond the fur. Lakes stopped traffic.

"Go to the trunk, Bill. Get the tarp, a blanket, and night stick."

Lakes laid the folded tarp on the pavement beside the dog.

"If she tries to bite me when I ease her on the tarp, gently put the nightstick between her teeth."

The dog tried to move, but couldn't. She made no effort to open her mouth. Lakes eased his hands under her, and Brand slid the tarp under the dog. Lakes took the blanket and laid it over the dog. He and Brand slid their hands under the tarpaulin. They carried her to the patrol car.

"Get in, Bill. Put on your seatbelt."

Lakes gently placed the tarp, dog, and blanket on Brand's lap, closed the door, and signaled the stopped traffic to move. He eased into traffic. He turned off the emergency light and drove within the posted speed to the veterinarian's office. They carried the tarp, the dog, and the blanket into the waiting room. The veterinarian answered the knock on his interior office door. Lakes and Brand walked in. They gently placed the dog on the examination table.

"Post 93, Car 953 to Post 93, signal 2 from the vet's office," radioed Lakes to the dispatcher.

"Copy your signal 2," replied the dispatcher. Lakes and Brand returned to their assigned patrol area.

"Whatya think goin' to happen to her?" asked Brand.

"Don't know. Too sad. Let's not think about her." He pointed ahead. "Gonna pull over that Chrysler with the broken taillight." Lakes eased the patrol car into position and turned on the pursuit light. The driver pulled over. While Lakes approached the driver, Brand took up position at the right rear bumper.

"Good evening, sir," Lakes said. "May I please see your driver's license and registration."

"Whatya stop me for?"

"Sir, your documents."

The driver fumbled for his wallet. With the license and registration in hand, Lakes said, "Mr. Jones, you were stopped for a defective taillight. We're going to give your vehicle a safety inspection. Turn on your windshield wipers, please. Sound your horn. Please put on your emergency brake. Put your car in gear and lightly touch your gas pedal. Turn on your headlights, please. Dim them, please. Your left turn signal . . . right turn signal . . . now turn your bright lights on again, and leave them on."

Lakes had walked forward and to the rear of the car as he had the driver turn things on and off. Done, he walked back to the driver's window to see if the high-beam indicator was working on the dash console.

"How are the rear turn signals, taillights, brake lights, license-plate light and reflectors?" Lakes asked Brand.

"Left taillight's broken. It's emitting a white light. The license-plate light isn't working," said Brand.

Lakes walked around the Chrysler and looked at the tires.

"Mr. Jones, your left taillight is broken, and your license-plate light is defective. I'm goin' to issue you an equipment-repair slip. You must get these defects corrected within seventy-two hours. Have the person who makes the repairs sign the slip. If you don't return the signed slip to the patrol post within seventy-two hours, you'll be issued a citation, and you will appear in court for these two violations. Do you understand the instructions as I've explained them to you?"

Jones nodded that he understood.

"Fine. Good evening, sir."

Back in their patrol unit, Lakes told Brand, "My method regarding either giving a written warning or a citation to appear in court for driving a vehicle that's unsafe is to count the equipment violations. If there are three or more serious violations, I issue a citation," said Lakes.

"What's a serious equipment violation?" asked Brand.

"That's where discretion comes in. Things such as a defective emergency brake, a defective muffler, and a smooth tire would qualify for issuing a citation for the driver to appear in court for operating an unsafe vehicle. But, don't do what I've heard about some police officers doing. Mind you, I said *police* officers, not state troopers," said Lakes.

"What's that?" asked Brand.

"It's when an officer arrests the driver because he used abusive language . . . that the driver didn't show the officer proper respect. Here's an example. An officer stops a vehicle for a defective headlight. He walks up and the driver says, 'Why in hell ya stop me? You damned cops are all alike . . . pickin' on us poor folks!' Well, about that time, the officer would order the guy to get out of his car. The chances are good the driver would be arrested, searched, and handcuffed."

"You mean he wouldn't first try to calm down the man? That's pretty drastic, isn't it?" asked Brand.

"And here's the clincher, Bill. The officer would really show him whose boss by calling a wrecker and having the car towed. So, the guy is out around 100 bucks for the tow and fine for the defective headlight."

"Seems like the fellow was arrested for disrespecting the officer . . . not for the violation. How can a police officer justify that?"

"What'd you do?" asked Lakes.

"Answer his questions. Try to calm him down."

The tour of duty continued. Brand watched Lakes stop several vehicles for equipment violations.

"Heard about a quota system . . . that you've gotta give so many tickets a day. Is that true?" asked Brand.

"Nope, not true. There's not a *specific* number you have to give, but you've gotta give *enough*."

"What's enough?"

"Depends on what you end up with each month if you've put forth reasonable effort. Safe number is around thirty. Anything above thirty's fine within reason."

"What's within reason?"

"Forty-five."

* * *

It was night. Lakes suddenly turned at a crossover on the interstate and then sped up to over ninety miles per hour.

"I'm after that third car ahead in the passing lane. We want to be behind those two vehicles that are also passing, so when they complete their passes we'll be in the passing lane directly behind the guy we're after. Let's hope he doesn't notice we're behind him."

The two vehicles in the passing lane drove back into the driving lane, leaving the violator the only vehicle in front of the patrol car. Lakes followed it at eighty-seven miles per hour, making sure he wasn't closing the distance between his squad car and the car he was pacing.

"That's all we need. We got him," said Lakes.

Lakes pressed the accelerator and eased to within 100 yards of the speeding motorist. The driver turned on his right turn signal, drove into the driving lane, and reduced his speed to sixty-five miles per hour. Lakes pulled up to the red Corvette's door and turned on his pursuit light. The driver immediately pulled onto the berm and stopped.

Lakes stopped car 953 ten feet behind and two feet left of the Corvette. He turned on his spotlight and high-beam headlights.

Brand stood his position at the right rear of the motorist's car. Lakes approached the driver. He stood slightly behind the driver's door. His right hand was empty. "Good evening, sir," he said. "May I see your driver's license and registration, please."

When these were turned over, Lakes said, "Mr. Cassidy, you still live at 1745 Liberty Street in Monroeville?"

"Yes, sir."

"Mr. Cassidy, the reason you were stopped is that you were traveling in excess of eighty-five miles per hour in a seventy-mile-per-hour zone. Because you live out of state, you'll be required to post an appearance bond. After you post your bond, you may sign a waiver. Whatever you choose to do, you'll be required to do it at the bonding station. The bonding station is approximately six miles further south. Drive about five and a half miles south and turn right at State Route 72. After a half mile, you'll see the police department on your left. That's the bonding station. We'll follow you to the station. Do you understand?"

"Yes, sir."

Lakes and Brand followed Cassidy to the station and then inside. Cassidy went up to the clerk. "I need to sign a waiver. Can't come back for court," he said to the court clerk.

"Let's see," said the clerk as he looked at the chart. The chart listed the amount required for each mile over the speed limit.

"Fifteen miles over," he said. "That'll be sixty dollars."

Cassidy paid cash, signed the waiver, and left.

"John," Lakes said to the clerk, "I'd like you to meet Bill Brand. He's our new trooper at the post. Bill, John Borg, night clerk of court."

"Glad to meet you," said Borg.

"Thanks, John. "It's good to meet you."

Lakes and Brand returned to the patrol post at five minutes to midnight. As they walked in, Lakes said, "After each tour of duty, you fill out your daily activity forms. You'll need to submit your arrests, warnings, accident investigations, and case investigations. Make sure they're complete, and then put them here."

Lakes put his seven written warnings and citation in the sergeant's report basket.

"We had a good shift, Bill. See you tomorrow afternoon at 3:30."

"Thanks, Ron. I look forward to it."

Lakes went to his squad car and drove home, while Brand went to the barracks, showered and slept.

*   *   *

The whistle's shrillness pierced Brand's ears at exactly six o'clock in the morning. He rubbed his eyes. He saw a trooper standing over him. "Get your ass out of bed," the trooper bellowed. "Don't ya know all men in this man's outfit are conditioned to get out of the sack at six o'clock? Move it, Brand!"

"Yes, sir."

"My name's Trooper George Jonsen. I work the 6:00 a.m. to 2:00 p.m. shift."

"Glad to meet you," replied Brand wearily.

"What time did ya get to bed?"

"About one."

"Hell, five hours sleep is enough for a young buck like you." Jonsen turned and walked from the barracks.

Brand made his bunk. He wondered what Jonsen's problem was. Five hours' sleep wasn't enough. Brand dressed in his sweat pants and shirt for his morning three-mile run. He opened the barracks door and saw Jonsen leaving the dispatcher's office.

"What in the hell is that outfit?" quipped Jonsen, staring at Brand's garb.

"I tend to think it speaks for itself," Brand said.

"Well, hell's bells, a joggin' suit! How many miles you gonna run today, Billy?"

"Just enough so I won't end up with a spare tire like the one you've got," retorted Brand to the surprised trooper.

"Well, we'll see what you look like when you get three service bars on your sleeve!"

Jonsen pointed to his three service bars that signified he'd been a trooper for fifteen years. No corporal or sergeant's stripes were on his sleeves.

When he got back from his run, Brand saw Trooper Lakes.

"Why you here so early, Ron?"

"Lieutenant called a meeting for seven thirty."

"Yeah? What's it about?"

"Don't know. Let's go in and find out."

Lakes and Brand took their seats with the other troopers.

The lieutenant entered the room. Someone said, "Ten-hut!"

"Seats, gentlemen," said the lieutenant. "I'll keep this short. This only looks like a meeting. It's not. There'll be no record of it. As you know, the legislature is considering us for a big pay raise. It's being passed around to all the posts to take it easy on ticketing state representatives . . . to take enforcement action only if it's absolutely necessary."

Brand looked at the lieutenant. He waited for him to make some wisecrack, so the troopers could laugh at the lieutenant's joke. He made no wisecrack. No one laughed.

"How much is the raise?" asked Jonsen. He rolled a cigar between his teeth.

"Ten percent!"

"Whoo-wee!" said Jonsen.

Brand looked at the other troopers. He saw them whispering. Brand looked at Lakes, but Lakes looked straight ahead and showed no expression. Brand looked at the lieutenant and raised his hand.

"Yes, Brand."

Brand stood. "Sir, we were taught at the academy never to show favoritism . . . to have our minds made up before we leave the squad car. Sir, this doesn't fit with what they taught us."

"Aw, for Christ sakes . . . forget what's said at the academy. You're in the real world now, Billy," said Jonsen. He laughed.

The other troopers didn't laugh.

"Sit down, Brand," said the lieutenant. He walked from the room.

Brand knew he'd made a mistake. He'd forgotten the lesson he learned at the academy. He'd stood out. He'd called attention to himself.

The post meeting ended.

"How can this be, Ron?" asked Brand.

"Sometimes you just have to roll with some of the low blows. You've gotta know where you personally draw the line. Otherwise, it'll be a slippery slope. You'll start to slide down that slope toward becoming a corrupt cop. Always remember this, Bill, we *are* the best law enforcement agency in the state."

Brand thought about the academy instructors. He'd admired them when he was being trained. He wondered what they would say.

* * *

Some days later, Jonsen stuck a letter in Brand's face. "Billy, here's a letter addressed to you. Looks like a woman's handwritin'. Must be from your mama," said Jonsen and chuckled.

"Thanks, George," Brand said and took the letter without acknowledging the man's ridicule.

Bill, I've been thinking about you. I hope all is well. Please remember to call me when you're done with your training. Victoria

Brand wasn't sure he knew what to make of that note.

* * *

"Car 953, Post 93 to Car 953."

"Go ahead, 93."

"Signal 10A on State Route 7 at County Road 91."

"You know what that is, Bill?" said Lakes.

"A possible fatal accident."

They surmounted the last hill.

"Call it in," said Lakes.

"Post 93, Car 953 to Post 93." This was the first time Brand had used the radio. He strove to sound professional and got the numbers right, but he was sure he spoke too loudly.

"Post 93 to Car 953, go ahead."

"Car 953 to 93, Signal 3. We're at the accident."

"Copy your Signal 3. Be advised the ambulance is en route."

"Copied, Car 953 out," replied Brand.

"Bill, put three flares on each side of the road. Then radio the post and ask for the next available wreckers. We need two."

Brand returned to Lakes. The ambulance arrived.

"Two injured women were taken to Central Hospital by a motorist," Lakes said after he checked out the accident.

"There's a man in that Ford who appears dead," said Lakes to the ambulance driver.

"Where ya want us to take him?" asked the ambulance driver. He looked at the old man sitting behind the truck's steering wheel.

"Central," said Lakes.

Brand was getting the 100-foot tape measure from the patrol car when he overheard the ambulance driver quip to his assistant, "Come on . . . let's get this old bastard outta here."

Brand walked to Lakes with the tape. A deputy sheriff drove by. The deputy, Lakes, and Brand returned nods.

"I see ya saw the deputy."

"Yeah," replied Brand.

Brand assisted Lakes. They took three measurements from the point of impact and also measured the width of the roadway.

"Hold traffic while I get pictures," said Lakes.

Brand walked to the traffic flow. He stood erectly and pointed his finger at an oncoming motorist. The driver looked at Brand. Brand looked at the driver, straightened his fingers, and showed the motorist the palm of his hand. The motorist stopped.

All the vehicles to its rear stopped.

Brand walked to the other side of the roadway and stopped traffic there.

The wreckers arrived. Lakes directed them to both vehicles.

The wrecker operators worked efficiently, and swept the roadway clear of metal and broken glass before they hauled the cars away.

Lakes and Brand completed the on-scene investigation.

"Start traffic. Smother the flares. Bring 'em back to the patrol car. Then we'll go to Central Receiving," said Lakes.

At Central a half-hour later, the troopers entered the emergency room and were directed to the driver. She couldn't talk because the doctor was stitching the length of her deeply gashed tongue.

The female passenger said to Lakes, "Officer, he just pulled right out in front of us! We were only going about forty." Lakes wrote his questions and her answers on the statement report form. She read the form and signed her name.

"Bill, let's go downstairs. I got a hunch about this one."

"What's the hunch?"

"That Ford's a stick shift. Guy could've had a heart attack or stroke while waiting for traffic to clear the intersection. Maybe his foot slipped off the clutch and brake. Ya noticed there weren't skid marks?"

Brand hadn't noticed and didn't answer, but he nodded.

"May we see the body, please, of the gentleman the ambulance brought in about forty-five minutes ago?" Lakes asked the attendant.

The attendant took the troopers to a side room. Brand expected to see a white sheet draped over a lifeless form on a metal cart. Not quite. On a bed, with a plaid, woolen blanket wrapped tightly around the body, was the dead man. The attendant took the blanket and the sheet from the corpse's head. Lakes and Brand looked at the large, light-blue bulge on the left side of the pale, white head.

"Whatya think, Bill?"

"Don't know, Ron. Maybe that lump could still be there whether he'd had a stroke or a heart attack. He was T-boned really hard."

"Just a minute," said the attendant. "Dr. Henry just walked by. I'll get him."

Dr. Henry looked at and pressed on the bulge.

"Could've had a heart attack or stroke before he went into the intersection. Or the reverse could be that he entered the intersection, caused the crash, and then had heart failure or a stroke," said Dr. Henry. "The coroner will likely be able to tell the difference. You might have to wait for that report."

After Dr. Henry left the room, Brand asked Lakes if there'd be an autopsy.

"Don't know. The old fellow failed to yield the right of way. Whether he was dead before the accident, or died because of the accident could be an issue if there's a lawsuit.

"I'll hold the report until we come back on duty. Then we'll try to get a written statement from the driver," said Lakes.

Before their tour of duty ended, Lakes cited a man for speeding in excess of seventy in a fifty-five-mile-per-hour zone.

"What you gonna do on your days off?" asked Lakes as he turned off the ignition.

"Think I'll head down to the university. I got a friend down there. After I see her, I'll go see my mom."

Lakes nodded. He didn't pursue Brand's reply.

Brand watched Lakes file the reports. Before leaving the post, Lakes introduced him to two troopers he hadn't met.

*   *   *

He thought about Mandy. He figured she'd be waiting up for him like she did every Friday night during his leaves from the academy.

Brand wondered if she was with someone else when he wasn't with her. He knew men looked at her.

He parked his truck and walked up the stairs to her apartment. Before knocking, he saw *Bill Brand* written on an envelope taped to her door. He opened it. In Mandy's handwriting it read, *I know, Bill, it's Friday night. Our relationship was special. I'm not here. Don't wait for me or phone me, Bill. Love, Mandy*

He thought, *a three-hour drive for this! She used past tense... "was"... Our relationship* was *special. I wonder who he is... probably a guy in law school.*

He wondered how she could do this to him. He wanted companionship, but there was no one. Brand left the city and began the two-hour drive to see his mother. He looked forward to seeing her. When he was sad, he always looked forward to seeing his mother.

* * *

During the drive back to the patrol post, he thought of Mandy. He was to go on duty shortly. He knew he'd better stop thinking about her and start thinking about the highway patrol. He idolized state troopers, and he idolized college professors. What Professor Whitcombe had written on his final examination confused him, and the note she sent him hadn't improved anything.

Something about her he didn't understand. He knew his coach had been upset when he'd quit basketball. Brand wondered if his coach asked her to do what she could to get him back to college and basketball. The coach was divorced. He wondered if the coach was dating Professor Whitcombe. He thought of her slender leg and her red skirt. He thought of her body. He thought of why she had written *Victoria* and not *Professor Whitcombe.* He thought of calling her, but he wondered if she were out of his league.

His thoughts turned to the humble, poor man from Mississippi. He thought of the guest speaker from the university who lectured at the academy about how the criminal-justice system in America is stacked against the poor.

* * *

"Today, Bill, we'll head south of the city to do some vehicle inspections. How'd your days off go?" asked Lakes.

"Fine. Spent time with Mom."

Lakes eased the patrol car off onto a wide berm where he could watch a stop sign while doing safety inspections.

"Post 93, Car 953 to Post 93 . . . Signal 3 at Nimrod Road and 894 for safety checks," Lakes said into the radio. Then to Brand, he said, "Just stand and watch how I do this. Don't ask any questions until the car that's stopped has left."

Brand nodded. He watched Lakes.

Lakes stepped onto the roadway and motioned a Chevrolet off the pavement and onto the wide-graveled berm.

"Good afternoon, sir." Lakes's voice was polite, but it had a tinge of dominance. Brand saw that he had used the same procedure approaching motorists he'd been taught at the academy. When Lakes approached the car, he had watched the driver for any movement that might suggest the driver or occupants could be reaching for a weapon. Lakes had quickly surveyed the front and back seats and floors to be sure no one was hiding.

"Sir, the reason you've been stopped is for failing to come to a complete stop at the Nimrod Road stop sign," said Lakes.

Brand hadn't noticed that the driver hadn't made a complete stop.

"Please know we're giving you a verbal warning for the stop-sign violation. Now that you're stopped, we're giving your vehicle a routine safety inspection. May I see your driver's license and registration, please?"

Brand saw Lakes kept the psychological as well as a physical advantage over the motorist by standing to the immediate rear of the driver's door of the motorist's car. Brand vividly remembered the example at the academy when the door was shoved open, and the unwary cadet was quickly pushed into a roadway full of make-believe traffic. Brand knew Lakes also stood in that position to lessen his chance of being shot. It would take more time and be more difficult for the motorist to fire back over his left shoulder. Brand remembered the psychological reason, too. The instructor had said, "The driver will immediately get out of his car if he wants to improve his chances of not getting a ticket. Standing outside the car puts the driver on par with the trooper. You don't want that. You want the driver seated and looking up and back at you."

The instructor had told the cadets, "If the driver does get out, firmly tell him or her to get back in the car. Tell the driver it's for his and your safety.

Their tours of duty ended. Brand showered and went to bed. He knew Jonsen's shift hadn't changed and would be on duty in the morning. He hoped Jonsen wouldn't wake him at six o'clock again.

Before he fell asleep, he wondered why the six-inch fold on the top sheet was so important. *Could the reason be if a person can't do little things right, then he probably can't do big things right, that starting one's day by doing a little thing right might set the day's tone for doing big things right?* As he settled closer to sleep he realized, *Everything in life matters, whether it's a big thing or a little thing.*

Again he wondered why Professor Whitcombe wanted him to call her. *The basketball coach could have asked her to do it.* Then he smiled. *Maybe she wants to quiz me about police training for a research project.* His last thought before he fell asleep was her red skirt just skimming her knee when she leaned back and put her heel on the second shelf of her bookcase.

3

THE NOVICE

GOOD AFTERNOON, SIR, may I see your driver's license and registration, please?" asked Brand.

He worked to keep his voice polite but firm. He watched the man's every move as he reached for his wallet. He'd been well schooled to watch the driver's actions, to be aware of any motion that might suggest movement toward a weapon. His heart pounded. This was his first traffic stop. Lakes stood at the right rear bumper where Brand had stood for three months, watching everything Brand did.

"Mr. Ralston," Brand said after he looked at the driver's license. He had practiced reading the license with just a glance, never taking his eyes off the driver. If he did, he might be killed. "Do you still live at 770 Wilson Avenue?"

"Yes, sir."

"Mr. Ralston, you were approached because you failed to make a complete stop at the intersection of Symmes and River Road. This, sir, is in violation of 953.833 of the Revised Code. You're going to be cited to court for this violation. Sir, court is Monday, Wednesday, and Friday at 10:00 a.m. and 1:00 p.m. What day and time next week would you like to appear?"

Brand's hands sweat. He grasped the citation book so tightly the top page showed the outline of his wet fingers.

The driver gave a disgusted, resigned sigh. "Wednesday at one. Can't I sign a waiver on this?" asked Ralston.

"You can, but you must appear before a clerk before your scheduled time in court next Wednesday. What's your occupation, Mr. Ralston?"

"Welder."

"Thank you, sir. Please remain in your car. I'm going back to write the citation."

Brand took two steps backward before he turned towards the patrol car. He put his left foot on the patrol car's front bumper to write the ticket. He periodically looked at the motorist.

Finished with the citation, Brand cautiously approached the driver. "Mr. Ralston, here's your copy of the citation, driver's license, and registration card. Sir, court is next Wednesday, the 24th, at one o'clock in the afternoon."

Ralston took the papers from Brand and drove away.

Brand watched the car drive off. "How'd it go, Ron?"

"You did fine," Lakes said. "A little too formal in what you said, but overall it was fine."

"What if he doesn't show up for court or sign the waiver?" asked Lakes.

Brand knew the answer. "The judge'll sign the back of the affidavit. It becomes a bench warrant. Then I go to the courthouse and get the bench warrant. I find him, arrest him, and take him in to post bond."

Lakes was silent.

Brand knew he'd made a mistake. He went through the procedure. He couldn't see it. Then he knew. It wasn't about the results of the driver missing his court date. It came before that. "Damn, I made a mistake, didn't I? I wasn't thorough enough, was I? I should've gotten more information about him. Should've gotten where he worked and his home and work phone numbers."

Lakes shrugged. "True, but he'll probably appear for court, or he'll sign a waiver and pay the fine. You'll develop a feeling about the ones who won't appear for court or sign the waiver."

Roles had changed. Brand had completed the three months as an observer. Now it was his time to be the active officer while Lakes observed him in action.

The weeks passed. Brand got more proficient at speaking to drivers. He had caught on to what Lakes saw on the road that made him focus on a particular car or driver. He heard nothing from Mandy. Professor Whitcombe made no more contact.

*   *   *

"Good afternoon, ma'am. My name is Trooper Brand. You were stopped for a routine equipment safety check."

He was in his final week with Ron before being "turned loose." Lakes watched him do safety checks.

The middle-aged woman wore a loose-fitting, low-cut blouse.

"Would you turn on your headlights, please? Try your dimmer switch, left-turn signal, right-turn signal, and sound your horn, please."

He walked to the rear of the vehicle. "Left-turn signal, right-turn signal. Now touch your brakes, please."

Brand put the metal clip of his clipboard directly under the license-plate bulb, so the rays from the bulb could shine on the metal clip and reflect back to him. Lakes showed him this technique to keep from kneeling down behind the driver's car to look at the bulb. He remembered well his caution that it would only take a split-second for the driver to slam the car in reverse and run over him. He needed to stay on his feet at all times. In this instance, the license-plate light was defective. Brand returned to the driver's door. The woman looked up and back at him.

"Please engage the parking brake. Now put your car in drive and give it just a little gas." The vehicle didn't move.

"Excellent. Now release the parking brake."

The woman leaned forward to reach the parking-brake release handle. He saw how the loose-fitting neckline of her blouse exposed her brassiere. The brassiere moved away from her chest while she anxiously grabbed the brake release. She unknowingly exposed herself. He instructed her to turn on the windshield wipers.

"You may turn off the wipers. May I see your driver's license and registration card, please?"

She searched her purse for her driver's license and registration card. She unknowingly exposed herself again. Brand saw that she wore a wedding band.

"Mrs. Wyatt, do you still live at 4278 Chestnut Street?"

"Yes."

"Mrs. Wyatt, I'm going to issue you a repair slip for your defective license-plate light. Please stay in your car. I'll return as soon as I write the repair slip. Please have the person who repairs the light sign the slip I give you. Then return it to the patrol station. You have seventy-two hours to complete the repair and get the slip to the station." Finished writing the repair slip, Brand handed it to Mrs. Wyatt along with her driver's license and registration card.

After several additional equipment repair slips were issued, he and Lakes returned to patrolling. As they drove, Brand had to tell Lakes what he had seen. "Remember the lady I gave the written warning for the defective license-plate light?"

"Yeah. What about her?"

"Well, it really surprised me . . . the view I got of her. Man, she was exposed!"

Lakes chuckled. "Happens about once a month during warm weather."

"We want to keep the drivers in their vehicles for their safety and for the psychological advantage of making them look up to us. No one ever said it was also the best position to catch a view of women who happen to be wearing loose-fitting or revealing blouses."

"What did they tell you in the academy about women?" asked Lakes.

"You mean in the sexual sense?"

Lakes nodded.

"They told us we're never permitted to follow up on a social contact with a woman we came in contact with while on duty."

Lakes nodded. "It's in the *Rules and Regulations*. Do ya know why it's in there?"

"My guess is they had trouble with men doing it."

Lakes said, "It's one of biggest discipline problems in law enforcement."

"What is?"

"The inability of officers to control their sex drives."

Brand remembered Professor Whitcombe telling them that certain professions—like law enforcement and the military—were careers that attracted men with high testosterone levels.

"How do they discipline them?" asked Brand.

"With troopers, it's usually penalty transfers to the other end of the state. It creates havoc with their families."

"You mean it's *married* men who get themselves in trouble on this?"

Lakes cocked an eye at him. "Bill, you can't be that naive!"

"Naw, just kiddin', Ron."

Lakes said nothing.

"How's the patrol feel about single men?" asked Brand.

"Our *Rules and Regulations* apply equally . . . single or married. This one asinine city police officer got himself in real hot water . . . mind you I said *city* police officer . . . not state trooper," said Lakes. "Winther was married. Had two kids. He worked the midnight to eight shifts. Here's what he did."

Lakes stretched to get more comfortable.

Brand figured Ron wished he were driving instead, that Ron looked forward to when they both would be "turned loose." Lakes said if all went well, he'd complete his six-month training period in three days. Brand waited for that moment, but he liked being with Lakes.

Other troopers told him Lakes was an outstanding state trooper, and he was lucky to have him as his field training officer. Primarily, though, Brand wanted to be on his own, to be a full-fledged state trooper.

"What about Winther?" asked Brand.

"Several months before you got here, we got a complaint from a woman. She was really ticked. Said a cop brought her sixteen-year-old daughter home at one o'clock in the morning. Dropped the girl off about a block from her house. Said she saw the front of the squad car from her kitchen window. The girl wouldn't tell her mom nothin'. The mother said her daughter just wouldn't talk about it. Said the daughter's boyfriend came the next day to pick up her daughter for a date."

"What'd the mother do?" asked Brand.

"Said she raised holy hell with the boy. Really lit into him. Accused him of all sorts of things. The girl pleaded for her mother to leave well enough alone. The mother said, how was she expected to leave well enough alone when her daughter got dropped off in a police car at one in the morning? The boy said the last time he saw her was eleven o'clock. He, too, now wanted to know what happened."

"What happened, Ron?"

"The girl had enough influence over the boy to keep him quiet. That really ticked off the mother. She really got uptight. Came out to the patrol post. To quote her, Bill, she figured, 'some cop was playing around with my daughter.'"

Brand drove the patrol car onto the interstate highway.

"Go ahead, Ron. I want to know what happened."

"Well, the lieutenant couldn't get any description of the squad car from the mother except the squad car wasn't white. He knew then it wasn't a state trooper vehicle. Anyway, an official complaint form was completed and signed by the mother.

"About two weeks after the complaint was filed, Trooper Vickus was on routine patrol. About midnight, he came across a city police car parked along Nimrod Lake. Vickus doused his lights, so if there was foul play . . . ya know, an officer being held hostage or something, he wouldn't be giving himself away. Vickus looked in the police car, and in the back seat, he saw a city police officer's ass over a woman. Vickus jotted down the number of the city police car and left. He figured the fellow was just getting a little extra on the side, so he'd just forget it. Ya know how close-knit law enforcement is. Most troopers won't squeal on another officer even when he's not a trooper."

"Yeah, I know, Ron."

"It bothered Vickus because he'd heard about the mother's complaint. He also has a teenage daughter. Next morning, he got the lieutenant alone and told him. The lieutenant, too, figured it wasn't state patrol's business, but he figured it could be related to the complaint he received from the mother. Anyway, the lieutenant got the city police car number from Vickus. He telephoned the mother to see if she had any additional information from her daughter, like a unit number on the police car. She had nothin' new.

"The lieutenant went down to the police department. He asked the chief if he'd received any complaints about one of his officers fooling around with women. The chief told him they were quietly investigating a complaint. Said the complaint consisted of the officer being accused of approaching couples making out in the city parks. Anyway, according to the lieutenant, this officer was accused of separating the couple. He'd tell the man to leave, that he'd take the woman back to her car or home in his squad car. The complaint went on to say that when the guy was gone, he'd tell the woman he would take her to her car or home . . . but not until she put out. If she didn't, he'd file charges against her and her lover for indecent exposure. The complainant said the officer talked about religion and questioned her about her faith in God. She said he told her he was not only a police officer for the city, but an officer in the service of God. The woman said his saying God told him to do this work is what really scared her. That's the gist of it."

"What'd the police department do?" asked Brand.

"When the lieutenant told the chief what his trooper saw the night before and we had a similar complaint, the chief sent the lieutenant to Internal Affairs. Internal Affairs told the lieutenant the officer in question wasn't aware a complaint had been filed. Anyway, a plan was formulated. A young state trooper from another district and his good-looking wife agreed to be decoys. They went into this parking area and started making out. Their rented car, the trooper, and his wife were all wired. Conversations were recorded and transmitted on a secure patrol frequency. Uniformed troopers hid nearby. Backup troopers patroled the area. They used a radio frequency not available to the city police."

"Car 953, Post 93 to Car 953."

"Car 953 to 93. Go ahead," answered Brand.

"Be advised of a personal-injury accident on County Road 8 and Highway 22. Ambulance en route."

"Copy on the personal-injury accident. En route."

Brand flicked the pursuit light switch. He increased his speed to eighty miles per hour.

Damn, thought Brand when he and Lakes arrived at the accident scene. "Post 93, Car 953 to 93, we're at the scene. Be advised: sheriff's office has a car here. They're investigating the accident."

Still, Brand parked and undid his safety belt. "We should get out and see if we can help," he said.

He felt odd making decisions about what to do because Ron was in the car. He wanted to do everything the way Ron would do it. Even though he was in charge, he worried about doing anything Ron might question.

After a brief survey of the scene, Brand and Lakes returned to their unit. "Car 953 to Post 93, be advised the deputy doesn't need any assistance. We're returning to routine patrol." Then Brand turned to Lakes and asked, "How come they're at so many of the accidents we get called on, Ron?"

"The sheriff wants re-elected, wants his department to get as much exposure to the public as possible. Some of us think the deputies monitor our radio frequency to hear our accident calls. Deputies aren't as well trained in investigating traffic accidents as we are, but they do a lot of things we don't have to do."

"What happened with the city police officer?" asked Brand.

"The plan was set, and sure enough, on the very first night, Winther drove up behind the plainclothes trooper and his wife. He shined his flashlight into the car and told the plainclothes trooper to come back to his squad car. He looked at his false identification and saw the picture of another woman and baby in the trooper's billfold. These were planted, of course. After some hemming and hawing, the trooper reluctantly said he was married . . . but not to the woman he was with. Winther, of course assumed this was the truth."

Brand appreciated Lakes using the word *assume*. At the academy an instructor wrote "assume" on the blackboard. He then wrote *ass/u/me*. The instructor said, "Anytime you assume anything, you may be making an ass out of you and me."

"Sounds like they laid a neat trap for him," said Brand.

"Winther walked the plainclothes trooper back to the car. He directed the woman to come to his squad car to be interviewed. He looked at her identification. She had on her wedding ring. Her identification was also false. Winther believed he had this woman right where he wanted her. He told the woman to stay in the squad car. He went back to the plainclothes trooper. Told him to go home to his wife and kid where he belonged. If he didn't, he said he'd call his wife and tell her what he saw and give his wife the name and address of the woman he was with. Then he told the plainclothesman to leave, that he'd escort the woman back to where she'd left her car. The trooper left. He radioed the other units on patrol to converge to within ten seconds of the location where his wife and Winther were located. Remember, Bill, everything was being recorded and transmitted."

Brand hadn't forgotten that salient point.

"Winther began his pitch by asking the woman if she believed in God. What woman wouldn't say 'yes' in this situation! Winther went on to say lust was one of the seven deadly sins, about how this woman should be so ashamed of her behavior what with having a husband and all. He told her he'd tell her husband what he saw and who her lover was because she needed to be punished for her sinful ways."

"My god, Ron, Winther's sick. He's mentally ill!"

"All this was being transmitted and recorded. The trooper's wife really played it cool and acted her part. She cried and begged Winther not to tell her husband because it'd mean the end of everything for her. She begged for forgiveness. Winther played right into our hands. He told the woman he'd say nothing if she could purge herself of her sinful ways. He said she could do that by promising that, after that night, she'd never again have sex with anyone except her husband. Winther said God had told him the only way for her to purge herself of her sinful ways and to prove she was sincere was if she'd make the promise while she's having sex with him. He said, 'I don't want to do this anymore than you do, but we're doing this for your salvation.'"

"Come on, Ron, you don't expect me to believe a line like that!"

"I didn't make this up. When you get back to the station tonight, look in the case file yourself. The recorded transcript is there, word for word. So the wife—and here's where she really did an acting job—she quietly said, 'Okay,' and she sank back into her seat."

"Ron, this guy's scary!"

He nodded vigorously. "She asked Winther what he wanted her to do. Winther said God wanted them to get in the back seat. He told her God wanted her to take off her blouse. That God wanted her to take off her bra. She said she would, but he'd have to remove his trousers at the same time, so they'd both be equally embarrassed. She slowly unbuttoned her blouse and then slowly reached behind her back to unsnap her bra."

"If they had everything on tape, why go this far?" Brand wanted to know.

Lakes nodded. "'Cause cops are armed, of course. Winther put his holster belt on the front seat, pushed his trousers and briefs below his knees, and that's when the camera flashed. The troopers hiding nearby had moved in. The trooper's wife buttoned her blouse."

"Man, did they ever have him cold. What'd they charge him with?" asked Brand.

"Nothing. They dismissed him from the force for misusing city equipment."

"What! You gotta be kiddin' me. You really mean they didn't arrest him?"

"Nope. The city police wanted to keep the whole thing quiet," said Lakes.

"One of my instructors said the divorce rate among police officers is higher than in any other profession . . . except for maybe the military. Do ya think that's true?"

"You bet I do," said Lakes. "What Winther did was bizarre. No officer would do anything close to that unless he's mentally off, but you're gonna be shocked with what goes on. If you want to have a happy life, Bill, pay attention to what's between a female's ears, and not what's between her arms and legs."

Brand didn't reply. He was silent because he was thinking about what Professor Whitcombe said the first day of class—a fourth of the population has some psychiatric illness and a half risk developing one. He changed the subject, asking Lakes how the patrol was planning to keep the sheriff's department from learning about the location of the patrol's accident calls.

Lakes said the plan was to code the main north-south highways with letters and the west-east highways with numbers. He said the dispatcher would look at the code sheet and then broadcast letters and numbers instead of the actual names of the highways.

4

THE ROOKIE

B RAND COMPLETED HIS SIX MONTHS' field training with a good report. He was "turned loose," finally a state trooper, and on his own.

Almost immediately, he found himself faced with a directive from General Headquarters that he didn't like. Troopers were required to check interstate rest areas for homosexuals twice during each tour of duty, to write the date, time, their name, and "Highway Patrol" on the Visitor's Sheet each time they checked the rest area. The times were changing, and behaviors considered lewd just ten years before, were being accepted by society. Homosexuality was one of these things. That men could love men openly was more or less accepted. The lieutenant said the directive was issued because the public complained homosexuals used the rest areas heavily. Brand had learned from Professor Whitcombe that homosexuals didn't choose their sexual identity. They were born that way. They had no choice in their orientation any more than heterosexuals. Brand also knew married men and women used the rest areas as a place to meet lovers who weren't their spouses. That, at least, was adultery, and still was considered wrong. But Brand needed to follow orders.

Brand parked his squad car on the berm of the interstate highway at midnight one night. He didn't want to drive into the rest area's parking lot because overhead street lights would give him away. He gently closed his car door. He walked up the small hill. Two cars were parked in the far corner of the parking area. A high overhead lamp illuminated the back seat. He saw a butt sticking up. He hoped it was kids. Those he could send home.

When he stood just outside the car, the person on his back looked up. He saw Brand. He pushed the person on top to the floor. They were both men. Brand turned on his flashlight.

"Please get your clothes on and get out of the automobile."

"Yes, sir," said the man on the floor.

Brand watched them closely.

"Both of you get out on this side of the car. Keep your hands where I can see 'em."

When both men stood outside the car, he said, "Identifications please. Take them out slowly." He reached for the first one. "Ryan Walsh. Still live at Route 2, Lafayette?"

"Yeah."

"Luke Tanner. And is this address correct in Winchester?"

"Yes, sir."

Brand saw Walsh eyeing him, but Tanner looked particularly scared.

"Gentlemen, you're under arrest for indecent exposure. You'll be required to post bond."

"Oh! God! No! No! You can't! I'll lose my church! Oh, God, No!" Tears streamed down Tanner's face.

Walsh didn't respond. He just watched Brand.

"Gentlemen, you have two options with your cars. One is I can have them towed for safe keeping. The other is you can lock them, leave them here, and come back and get 'em later. If you leave your cars here, you're responsible for them."

"I don't know what to do," answered Tanner. He looked at Walsh.

"I'll lock mine up," said Walsh "All right. I will too," said Tanner.

"For the report, Mr. Walsh, what's your occupation?"

"Truck driver."

"Mr. Tanner, your occupation?"

"I'm ... I'm a minister." Tears still streamed down his face.

Brand sat Walsh in the front seat and Reverend Tanner in the back seat of his squad. Walsh sat impassively. As Brand was writing down their places of employment and their work and home phone numbers,

Reverend Tanner rocked back and forth with his hands cupped in front of his face.

"What you doing?" asked Brand.

"Praying. Can't you give me a break? I'll lose my life's work." In his cupped hands, Brand saw a small silver-and-black crucifix.

"Sir, you should've thought about the consequences of your actions before you got into that car. You, if anyone, should know better, you should. How could a man of God do such a thing?"

Brand winced when he heard those words come from his own mouth. Regardless of his own beliefs, his duty was to enforce the law. It wasn't his job to pass judgment. He knew these men didn't choose their sexual orientation any more than he chose his. He also believed that very soon the men's behavior would not be considered unlawful.

"Officer, even we Ministers of God are human."

"I know, Reverend Tanner," Brand said gently. "Please accept my apology. I shouldn't have said that."

Brand thought of Professor Whitcombe. He knew she'd say, "*I told you so, Bill. Still like being a cop now? Still think quitting college and quitting basketball was smart? If they'd been a man and a woman, you wouldn't have arrested them, now would you have, Bill?*"

"Post 93, Car 833 to 93. I'm at the south rest area on the interstate en route sheriff's department with a Mr. Walsh and a Reverend Tanner for bond posting. Charges are indecent exposure. Their vehicles are locked at the rest area."

"This is Post 93. Copy, 833."

The bond was fifty dollars apiece. Brand left the booking area immediately after he submitted the arrest forms. He drove back to the patrol post.

"What happened, Billy . . . with the queers, I mean?" asked Jonsen.

"Nothing much. Just saw 'em with their pants down rubbing each other."

"Then what?"

"I told 'em to put on their clothes."

"Then what?"

"I got their identifications?"

"Quit beating round the damn bush. What in hell did you do?"

"I arrested them for indecent exposure."

"How come you didn't take them for sodomy?"

Brand stared at Jonsen. The man was enjoying this way too much. "I didn't see penetration. Damn, the more I think about it, the more I wish I hadn't arrested them at all. I wish I'd just let 'em go."

"What! You've got the best pinch going this month!"

"Yeah, sure. One guy's a minister. I ruined his life."

Jonsen hooted. "You didn't ruin it. He did. What'd they teach you in that college, boy? You're in the real world now, Billy. The real world isn't their world. Those professors spent their whole lives with their noses in books. They wouldn't know how to pour piss out of a boot with instructions on the heel. They hire people to clean their houses, cut their lawns, fix their leaky faucets. All they ever did was go to school, get a tax-supported, gravy job for life, and put 'Doctor' in front of their names. Hell, they ain't even *real* doctors, just overeducated, overpaid, and overprotected pompous sonsabitches. Professors screwed up your head!"

"I had some great professors, George, people who knew a lot more than only how to be professors. They knew a lot more than you. You and I'll just have to agree to disagree on how we see the value of professors and the value of a college education. I love the highway patrol, but I've gotta figure out a way to finish college, too."

"That's bullshit, Billy. Man, how can you be so damn naive? Your mind's screwed up. College did that to you. You think too damn much. Look at it this way. Those guys were horny, so they went to a place where they could get laid. Our rest area. Then they did it, right? Man, they had it comin'. They really did. If I'd been in your shoes, I'd've arrested them for sodomy."

"What! You tellin' me you would've arrested them for a felony even though you didn't see penetration?"

"Hell, yes! It's not like they weren't going to do it. You just got there too soon."

"What if it had been a man and a woman? Would you've arrested them for sodomy?"

"Hell, no. That's different. I'd watch a bit, then I'd let 'em go."

"But how's that different?"

"You *are* an idiot! The goddamned Bible says it's wrong. Men ain't supposed to have sex with men, and women shouldn't have sex with women."

"What about adultery?"

"What in the hell does adultery have to do with what we're talkin' about?"

"'Thou shall not commit adultery—it's one of the Ten Commandments. The Bible says it's wrong, too. I've checked out men and women making out in rest areas who are married, but not to each other. They're committing adultery, and I could've arrested some of them for indecent exposure . . . some even for sodomy, but I didn't."

Jonsen gave Brand the finger and said, "You think too goddamned much, Billy Boy." He turned and walked away.

Brand knew he wouldn't have arrested them if they'd been a man and a woman. He knew what he did was wrong even if the law said what he did was right. He also knew he couldn't undo what he'd done.

Brand knew if Professor Whitcombe had seen what he'd done, she'd say, "*Bill, I explained in class that male homosexuals don't choose their sexual preference. You were in that class, Bill. You knew better. Why, Bill, why did you do that? Why did you destroy the minister's life?*"

*   *   *

"Car 833, Post 93 to Car 833."

"Car 833 to 93."

"Be advised of a reported fatal on code 4 at C. Repeat code 4 at C."

"Copy on the reported fatal on code 4 at C. En route."

It didn't take Brand long to arrive at the location. "Post 93, Car 833 to 93. Be advised I'm at the reported fatal," said Brand.

Bystanders had gathered, but they kept a ten-yard distance from the crumpled automobile. A blanket had been draped over a portion of the car. Brand thought it was over the driver's door, but the vehicle was so crushed and distorted he couldn't be sure. He walked to the car and pulled back the blanket.

A man sat in what had been the driver's seat. His head was down. Most startling, his left eyeball and the pinkish-white optic nerve hung ten inches from his eye socket. The man's left leg stuck through the left side of the crumpled automobile. His trouser was torn away. His skin was cleanly peeled off as well. Brand saw leg muscles. He wondered why there was no blood. He put back the blanket.

A semi-tractor and trailer lay on its side. Another semi-tractor and trailer, that one upright, had gone into the ditch. Coiled steel from one of the trucks was scattered over the two-lane highway. He walked back to the huddled people.

"No one else injured, officer," a short, chubby man in a red plaid shirt said to Brand. "I'm the driver of that truck." He motioned his head toward the overturned semi-tractor and trailer.

"Was he alone?" asked Brand.

"Don't know. Guess so," said the truck driver. Brand walked back to the automobile. He saw no signs of anyone else in the crumpled wreckage.

When he returned to the crowd, another man said, "I'm the driver of the semi in the ditch."

Brand looked at the two trucks, then at the automobile. The car was smashed so badly Brand couldn't tell the front from the back.

"What happened?" asked Brand.

"I was drivin' east about forty," said the one truck driver.

Brand knew his slow speed was caused by the uphill grade.

"This fellow," the truck driver said, pointing to the blanket covering the dead man, "passed me. Must've been doin' eighty. Passed me right in front of that truck over there."

The trucker motioned to the overturned semi-tractor and trailer that had strewn the coiled steel over the roadway.

"When he tried to pull back in, the semi comin' downhill smacked him real good. Drove him right back into me. We just kind of . . . squashed him. That's it . . . just squashed him."

The roof of the car was peeled back from the windshield to the trunk. Brand climbed on top of the twisted wreckage. He put his knees on the top of the back of the driver's seat. He reached under the dead man's armpits, locking his arms with his hands. He hugged the dead man. The left side of his face was snug against the right side of the dead man's face. Brand's gaze moved left and down, fixed on the hanging eyeball and the long, pinkish-white optic nerve that kept the eyeball attached to the dead man's face.

He pulled. The body moved a few inches upward, but it seemed stuck. He moved his knees closer, gripped the man tighter and pulled harder. The body lunged upward, then stopped. The eyeball swung around the dead man's face, and the optic nerve touched Brand's lips. The eyeball tapped the right side of Brand's face, causing him to drop the man. He watched the dead man's eyeball swing slowly back and forth.

I've gotta get him outta here. Traffic is blocked for miles in both directions, thought Brand. The tow trucks had arrived but couldn't take the car with the man inside.

Brand reached down between the front of the seat and the dead man's back, wondering if the moisture on his hand was blood or urine. *He's got a seatbelt on,* Brand said to himself. He slowly pulled out his hand and looked at it. It was wet. Not blood.

Brand wiped his hand on the blanket. He reached into his pocket for his penknife. With the blade open, he eased his hand back into the wetness, searching for the seatbelt. He found it and cut it.

Again he hugged the dead man's body, this time leaning his face away from the dead man's head to avoid the swinging eyeball. He pulled. The body surged upwards. The eyeball arched upward but missed Brand's head. Then the ambulance attendants helped him put the dead man into their vehicle. It slowly drove away.

A bystander helped Brand by holding the end of his tape measure as he finished taking down information about the scene. Then the twisted automobile was winched onto a truck bed. A heavy-duty wrecker was already working to get the upright tractor and trailer out of the ditch and righting the overturned semitractor and trailer. The wrecker drivers and helpers cleared coiled steel from the roadway. Finally Brand was able to motion the stopped traffic to move past the accident site. He took written statements from the two truck drivers and drove them to a truck stop. He needed information about the dead man to complete his investigation.

The undertaker at Calvert Funeral Home opened the locked door when he knocked and identified himself. "Come on down. We're just getting ready to embalm him. Looks like he was put through a meat grinder!"

Brand looked at the naked dead man lying on an inclined porcelain table with a wooden block under his neck. A small piece of brown rubber sheet covered his privates.

"His billfold's on the counter over there," said the undertaker.

Brand nodded. He looked through the billfold for the driver's license, encountering a picture of the dead man, his wife, and three children. He saw the undertaker put on rubber gloves and pick up a scalpel. He made a three-inch incision in the right shoulder near the neck of the dead man and probed the incision with his finger.

"Ouch! Dammit! The sonofabitch bit me!" yelled the undertaker. He jerked his finger from the incision and shook it. The undertaker's helper, standing on the other side of the corpse, laughed.

"What happened?" asked Brand.

"Ah, he's so busted up one of his broken bones jabbed me. I'm going have to embalm him in sections—a helluva job."

"Please take a look at this," said Brand. He opened the man's billfold. "Here's a picture of him, his wife, their three kids. Don't ya think you owe his body a little respect? Whatcha doing calling him a sonofabitch?"

"How long you been a trooper, son?" asked the undertaker.

Brand shifted his weight. "This is my first fatal since I've been on my own."

The undertaker nodded. "May I ask how old you are?"

"Twenty-one."

The man nodded again. "I've been embalming people for over thirty years, son, and this is one of the worst I've seen. I meant no disrespect to him. I'd have gone nuts long ago if I'd thought about a body as a person, what he or she was and did, and who would be missing him or her. My lousy attempt at humor is my way of coping. Please accept my apology."

"I'm sorry. I apologize, too. I'm such a rookie," said Brand.

"Lotta cops get hardened to the point they don't feel anything anymore. Don't become one of them," said the undertaker. "Better to stay human and feel than become an automaton."

Brand nodded. "I got the information I need on him. Could I use your phone?"

The undertaker pointed to the wall phone. Brand gave the information about the dead man to the patrol post dispatcher.

Because the driver came from out of state, information would be sent to the driver's home area. The dead man's local police force would be informed and would notify his wife. Brand was relieved he wouldn't have to do it.

* * *

Brand resumed regular patrol. He eased his patrol car into the rest area on the interstate highway, noticing that most of the cars in the parking area had local licenses. He saw no women or children. When he walked into the men's restroom, he saw a man standing at the urinal. He also saw the small hole at eye level someone had cut in the green Plexiglas. Guys used the peephole as a lookout for other homosexuals who drove into the rest area.

Back outside, Brand walked to the drinking fountain. Most of the cars had left. He signed the visitor sheet, returned to his squad car, and headed south. He thought about what he'd done to Reverend Tanner, and wondered if he really had lost his church. He knew he would never forgive himself if he had. He also knew he could never make up for what he'd done.

"Post 93, Car 833 to Post 93, I'll be out of service at the O.K. Cafe." Brand parked his squad car and locked it. He put the keys in his right hip pocket, where he always put them. At the academy, it was stressed to the cadets to put patrol car keys in the same place so that, in an emergency, the trooper wouldn't be fumbling around trying to find his keys.

Brand entered the restaurant, quickly surveying the people and vacant seats, looking for a booth where he could have his back to a wall and see the entry door and cash register. He washed his hands before taking his seat. This, too, was taught at the academy.

He remembered the instructor saying ordering first and then going to the bathroom could be a major mistake. *"You must never leave your coffee, water, and food unguarded. If you do, someone could put a drug in your drink or spit on your food.*" He remembered the instructor saying, "*Be careful, gentlemen, be very, very, careful.*"

Brand followed the etiquette rules taught at the academy, recalling further instructions. "*When drinking from a glass, always put your thumb on the left side and three fingers on the right side of the glass. The little finger goes under the glass. The little finger will prevent the glass from slipping through your fingers and spoiling your uniform.*"

Brand ate his meal, then asked for the check. He knew what his bill should be. The waitress had charged him half price.

He approached the cash register and whispered to the female cashier, "I'd like to pay full price, please."

"I'm sorry," said the cashier, "the owner says police are to eat at half price."

"I know, but I wanna pay full price."

"I can't. The owner . . . he'd get mad . . . he'd fire me."

It was time to shut up and wished he hadn't raised the issue with the cashier. He should have just made sure to leave the right amount on the table. Other customers waited in line to pay their checks. He knew policemen and troopers ate at the O.K. Cafe, and they'd be upset with him if he ruined their "meal ticket."

He took the change and went back to his booth. There he left the rest of the tab and a tip. Even if the owner didn't get the money, he was paying his way as he should.

* * *

"Post 93, I'm driving by the area you advised," radioed Brand to the dispatcher. "Can't find it."

A week had passed. Brand received his second dispatch to investigate a fatal accident, but he couldn't find it.

Dispatch gave him the location again. "Right, I've driven by this area twice . . . no accident. I'll try again using my spotlight."

Brand slowly drove his patrol car along the two-mile stretch. It was one o'clock in the morning. He drove at five miles per hour. He rotated his spotlight from the berm to the center of the roadway. He looked for some evidence a car had been involved in an accident . . . that it'd been moved before he'd arrived. He was looking for bits of glass or tire tracks. He entered a sharp S curve and continued to shine his spotlight along the berm. Finally Brand stopped his patrol car, being careful not to get too close to the edge.

He saw several small pieces of limestone gravel on the roadway and small, white scratch marks on the dark pavement where a tire had tried to brake but had slid over the limestone. These marks were perpendicular to the curve of the black, asphalt roadway and gave him a clue where to look for the car. He walked to the edge and looked down into the deep ravine.

"Post 93, Car 833 to Post 93. I located the accident. It's at a sharp S curve. The vehicle is sitting upright with the headlights on about 150 feet down at the bottom of a ravine. I'll be off the radio for about half an hour. Going down to investigate."

Brand opened the trunk of his patrol car to grab a rope and first-aid kit. He tied one end of the rope around the front bumper of his car and eased himself down the steep embankment. While lowering himself, he saw how no one could've seen the accident from the highway even with the car's headlights on.

He asked himself, *Who called the highway patrol to report the accident if I couldn't even find it?*

He paused in his descent to slap his neck. "Damn bugs," he whispered. Mosquitoes swarmed.

The doors of the car were closed. The key was in the ignition, and the headlights were on. No one was in the car. He saw a deep dent on the left front of the hood. Before the scene got trampled, he looked for tire tracks and footprints around the automobile. There were none. He thought, *It's as if the hand of God placed it here.* He looked upward, shining his flashlight high into the trees. Then he knew what happened.

The driver lost control on the sharp turn, locked his brakes, scratched the pavement with the stones between his tire treads, flew off the embankment, tore off the bark when he hit that tree limb, and the car landed here.

He was amazed at the tremendous distance the car had traveled through the air.

But, where was the driver? Had there been passengers? They could be wandering around half dazed.

He cupped his hands and yelled, "Yo, anyone here!"

He slapped another mosquito biting his shoulder through his uniform shirt. A small spot of blood marked the spot. He meticulously picked off the mosquito. *I should've let it bite me rather than get blood on the uniform,* he thought.

He continued looking for signs of a driver or passengers.

There were none. Seatbelts were unbuckled. He knew he should get back to his squad car and call for help.

He looked at his uniform. Briars were stuck in his trousers. Scratches marred his spit-shined leather holster, handcuff case, and shoes. He decided to walk through the brush to see if he could find something or someone. Even if the driver had been alone, he had to be somewhere.

He walked fifty paces away from the vehicle and started to circle the vehicle, pushing his way through the underbrush. Mosquitoes attacked him voraciously.

Three-fourths of the way in his circuit of the car, he saw a white object between him and the car lights. He killed mosquitoes biting his neck, face, back, and arms. He heard nothing but their continuous hum. He walked toward the white object.

A man, naked to the waist, lay face down on the damp leaves. Brand unsnapped his holster strap and touched the man's neck. The skin was clammy. No pulse. He placed his left hand under the man's bare shoulder and turned him on his back. Brand looked at the bearded face and the pasty, half-opened eyes. Neither mosquitoes nor mosquito welts stood out on the dead man's skin. They wanted Brand.

He reached under the back of the dead man's jeans and felt a billfold. He opened it. *Carl W. Clansky, 1137 Seneca Avenue. In case of emergency, notify Loretta Clansky, same address. A phone number was listed.*

"Post 93. Car 833 to Post 93."

"Post 93 to Car 833, go ahead."

"Here's the situation. Located a body. Deceased is Carl W. Clansky, 1137 Seneca Avenue. Saw no evidence of additional people. Dispatch an ambulance and advise them to bring 200 feet of rope, mosquito dope, a body basket, and a strong man. Advise them to dress in hunting-type clothes. To bring flashlights. Let 'em know I'll be standing by waiting for 'em. The tow truck can wait until daylight. It'll need to be a heavy-duty tow with three hundred feet of cable and chain at least. Tell the tow-truck driver to bring lots of mosquito repellent, a chainsaw, and that three men might be needed to get the vehicle up to the highway. Who reported the accident?"

"A woman called the patrol post, but refused to give her name," said the dispatcher.

While waiting for the ambulance, he continued his on-scene investigation. The ambulance arrived with no mosquito dope, no extra man, and no body basket.

The ambulance driver and Brand struggled, but they couldn't get the dead man up the steep embankment.

"Want a hand?" yelled the wrecker operator from up top.

Brand looked up through the trees to the highway and yelled, "Thank god you didn't wait until daylight. You bet we need help. Got anything we can put a body in? Weighs about 200 pounds."

"Got a container we put wrecker parts in. You want me to lower it?"

"Yeah, and put the chainsaw in it, too."

The cable, basket, and chainsaw bumped down to the bottom of the ravine. Brand and the ambulance driver lifted Mr. Clansky into the wrecker's metal basket, and Brand cleared a path with the chainsaw ahead of the basket climbing carefully as he went. In this way, the basket and body were winched up to the highway, and Mr. Clansky's body was loaded into the ambulance.

Two hours passed. The wrecker, with some difficulty, managed to drag up the car and hauled it away. Brand asked the dispatcher if the next of kin had been notified.

"Negative. There's no answer at the residence . . . tried telephoning several times."

"I'll stop by the wife's address on my way in and notify her if she's home," radioed Brand.

It was breaking daylight when he approached Seneca Avenue. He saw a tall, slender woman guiding a young child into the house identified in Mr. Clansky's wallet.

"Be advised: next of kin just arrived home," radioed Brand to the dispatcher. "The deceased . . . is he at Central Receiving?"

"Negative. He was, but he's already been taken to Baughman's Funeral Home."

"Autopsy?" asked Brand.

"That's a negative," replied the dispatcher.

Brand said he'd be out of radio contact at the Clansky residence, that he'd be advising Loretta Clansky of her husband's death.

Brand swallowed hard. He asked himself if he could tell this woman her husband was dead.

He knocked. The woman opened the door. She was penetratingly beautiful—green eyes and auburn hair.

"Mrs. Carl Clansky?" he asked softly.

"Y-yes," she replied and stepped back from the door.

"May I come in?"

She nodded.

Brand followed her into the living room, his Stetson in his hand. "Mrs. Clansky, my name's Trooper Brand of the Highway Patrol." He paused. "Do you have a neighbor or friend I could call to have come over?"

"Wait a minute," the woman said, holding up a hand. "Wait until I'm sure my daughter's upstairs."

When she returned, Brand started again. "Mrs. Clansky, I'm very sorry, but your husband was involved in a fatal accident several hours ago."

The woman gasped, and a shaky hand came up to her mouth. "Where's he? I want to see him."

"He's been taken to Baughman's Funeral Home." Brand helped her to a chair. "May I telephone someone for you?"

She didn't respond. He was thankful the child remained upstairs. "May I . . ." he said softly, pointing to the phone.

"My sister, please. We just left her house." She stared but seemed to be looking nowhere. Her expression reminded him of the dog's look when hit by the car on his first duty day.

"Her number?" asked Brand.

"Her name's Hollindale. The number's on the counter, by the phone. They live a few blocks from here. Can I see him?"

"Thank you. I'll call her now." He didn't answer her regarding her husband.

The woman's sister and brother-in-law arrived within a few minutes. Brand quietly left them to their grief. He spoke with Mrs. Clansky's sister's husband in the yard. In a low voice, he explained the accident to him. The man said his sister-in-law had been having marital problems. She and her husband had been at a bar. They fought, and her husband sped away, leaving his wife there. The sister and brother-in-law had picked her up and took her to their house where her daughter was staying overnight. That was why she wasn't home when the patrol tried to reach her by telephone.

Brand drove toward the funeral home. He visualized the widow's face. His thoughts went back to the academy to the lecture on bereavement for widows of slain patrol officers. The lecturer had been a guest psychologist. He'd said:

"The widow asks herself if she's done all she could do for her husband when he was alive. It's possible that feelings of self-doubt concerning the dead husband be directed toward suicidal thoughts. She's lonely and without direction. Self-inflicted death may be viewed as a form of punishment for not being fully devoted to her husband or suicide may be seen as a reward in the sense that, through her death, the wife will join her husband. The initial reactions are usually extreme yearning or desire for the husband. Physiological reactions can be loss of weight, diarrhea, constipation, headaches, and restlessness."

Brand recalled he ended his lecture with the statement, *"All troopers have the obligation to teach their wives how to be widows."*

Brand drove to the parking lot of Baughman's Funeral Home. He saw no lights except what escaped from around a Venetian blind. He rang the doorbell at the rear of the funeral home. A buzzer sounded. Brand opened the door into a garage. He walked up the ramp to the door where there was a small light.

The door was locked. Brand knocked.

"Just a minute," came a voice from within. "Who is it?"

"Trooper Brand, Highway Patrol."

The door opened.

"Hi, I'm Bill. I need some information on Mr. Clansky to complete my report. Can I get it?"

He entered the small room full of equipment and Carl Clansky's body. Brand found the driver's license and began to write the information on the accident report. He noticed the undertaker had made a deep incision into the extreme-upper-inside thigh of Carl Clansky's right leg. Yellow flesh visible in the incision didn't bleed. With his rubber-gloved finger, the undertaker searched for the femeral artery, and cut it. Dark blood flowed over Carl Clansky's scrotum onto the inclined, porcelain table to a drain.

"Where's the blood go?" asked Brand.

"City sewer. What killed him?" asked the undertaker.

"Car flew off the highway. Wasn't wearin' a seatbelt. Was thrown through his open window when the front of his car hit a big limb. I figure when his shoulders started out the window the left side of his head was blocked by the top of the window frame. That snapped his neck."

"Seems logical. Look how this side of his neck's swollen," said the undertaker. "It's broken there. The coroner will be in before church. He'll probably agree."

Brand wondered, but didn't ask, why he was embalming the body before the coroner viewed it.

While the undertaker talked, Brand saw him close Clansky's jaw with the palm of his hand, staple a wire in the upper and lower gums, and tightly twist the wire to lock the jaw closed.

"Do ya smell somethin' strange . . . something kinda sweet?" asked Brand.

"Yeah."

"What is it . . . a combination of blood and alcohol?"

For a moment the undertaker didn't answer. Then he said, "I believe so . . . but don't quote me."

"Okay, just save some blood for me."

Brand handed the undertaker a small test tube with a rubber stopper. Troopers used it to get blood samples from drivers killed in traffic accidents. The undertaker got a large metal syringe and with both hands jammed the needle deep into Carl Clansky's chest.

Brand returned to the patrol post to complete his report.

He finished the report. He showered, changed uniforms, and returned to his assigned patrol area.

*   *   *

Three months passed since Carl Clansky had been killed. Brand tried to think of an excuse for meeting Loretta Clansky again. He didn't want to refer to the accident or show up in his uniform. He chose the only alternative he thought available to him. He telephoned Loretta.

* * *

Brand knew Loretta could tell the patrol he'd called her, and he knew seeing a woman socially who he had dealt with professionally was violating regulations. He was following up on a female encountered in the line of duty. But he wanted to see her, he wasn't even sure why. Maybe it was that she was the first person to whom he'd given a death notification. Maybe he felt sorry for her and her child. Maybe it was something else.

"Come in, please." She spoke to Brand in a soft, pleasant voice. He heard her deep accent. He hadn't remembered her accent the first time he'd met her.

He thought, *She's wearing a dress. Mandy wouldn't dress like that. Mandy would be wearing faded jeans and a loose-fitting sweatshirt as she so often did and likely without a bra.*

Loretta didn't want to go out for the evening. She said three month's mourning was too soon to be seen with a man. Instead, she invited him into the living room and sat across from him. She told him she hadn't fixed a steak dinner since her husband's death, but Brand visiting presented her an excellent opportunity to fix one. Brand thought momentarily about her logic, then thought about the price of steak.

They talked. Loretta spoke of how she wanted to avoid the divorcee or widow syndrome, and she'd been heading toward the one when her husband's death handed her the latter. She talked about her friend back home, an attractive woman whose husband was killed in the mines, and how she was now an alcoholic and a party girl.

"How do you know she's an alcoholic?" asked Brand.

The woman shrugged. "You'd only have to see her to know. Wendy was widowed three years ago. She has a baby. Doesn't want a job. Her welfare, food allotment, and extra income are big enough. She's ... gettin' by. I talked to her. Oh, Lord, did I talk. I told her she oughta get a job. She'd just laugh and say she was having a blast bein' single. She dates. Come to think of it, she dates a lot."

Brand wondered about Loretta's marriage. He thought about her brother-in-law's comment on the night of her husband's death. Marital problems.

"Well, Bill, if you'd look at her closely, you'd see what kinda blast she's havin'. Those small red lines are beginning to show in her eyes ... really a shame."

Brand was relieved he wasn't offered a beer, just talk.

The evening ended. He wanted to see her again and considered the dichotomy between Mandy and Loretta. Loretta was a country girl, a widow with a child. Mandy was a junior in college and middle class. Loretta hadn't graduated high school and could've been on welfare. She, her husband, and her child had come to town to find work. Loretta fascinated him.

He hadn't heard from Mandy and wondered if he ever would again. Often, his desire would rise to a point where he'd reach for the telephone or stationery, but he remembered the academy instructor saying that troopers didn't lower themselves to chase women, that they had sensitive and supportive natures and were not ashamed to be men. Troopers were men with a commanding presence.

Brand questioned himself. He knew he'd broken a patrol regulation by following up on a female he'd met in the line of duty. He wondered if a man was someone bright enough to make decisions on his own and not blindly follow rules. Did the *Rules and Regulations* exist only as guidelines? Were troopers supposed to use good judgment and not rely solely on the *Rules and Regulations*?

He thought of his two-day leaves from the academy when he drove to Mandy's apartment for their Friday nights together, thought, too, of their agreement that they were too young to be in an exclusive relationship. Her body always felt like satin, and that made him wonder about Loretta's body. Was someone else with Mandy? And then his thoughts backed up to Victoria. Brand re-assessed what he was doing and resolved he would chase no woman.

5

THE AWAKENING

B RAND, WE NEED YOU," said the lieutenant.
"Ready, sir. What for?"
"Basketball."

That had been a rather unexpected response. Brand listened as the lieutenant said the highway patrol was conducting tryouts to locate the best players in the state for a benefit basketball game against the state's professional football team. The football team was in offseason and wanted to play the highway patrol in a benefit basketball game. The lieutenant stressed the patrol's honor was at stake, that they didn't want to lose that game, benefit or not.

Brand traveled to the tryouts with troopers Ruzan and Jonsen. Though Brand was rusty and moved a little sluggishly on the court, he thought maybe he had shown enough of his stuff to get on the team. After tryouts, they stopped at the Dew Drop. Brand knew both Ruzan and Jonsen thought he was naive. Ruzan and Jonsen were married, but they left Brand standing alone in back of the barroom and sauntered up to a table where two women sat. In just a few minutes they were sitting with the women and buying them drinks. They danced with them. After a while they returned to where Brand was. They complained of being tired from the basketball tryouts and dropped off Brand at his apartment. Brand knew they were going back to the Dew Drop because they talked too much about how tired they were and about how they were looking forward to getting home and going to bed.

*   *   *

The lieutenant said to Brand, "Here's something for you to follow up on."

Brand read the entry on the post log:

Ruby West of 1617 Benton Drive, Apartment D, reference an individual in street clothes who approached her in the East Side Foods parking lot at approximately five o'clock in the afternoon. He showed her a badge, advised her that he was a detective, and said that she was approached because her car fit the description of a recently reported stolen Cadillac. He asked to see her driver's license and registration, then asked for and received her telephone number. The individual then looked at the bolts on her license plates, advised her that her car was not the one reported stolen, and said she could be on her way. She stated she had an unlisted phone number and has now been receiving telephone calls from someone. She can hear breathing but the caller says nothing. She believes it to be the detective who approached her in the East Side Foods parking lot. Complaint is assigned to Trooper Brand for follow up.

The lieutenant said, "Don't look so surprised, Bill. We're already sure the person who said he was a detective wasn't a trooper. If it'd been, I would've taken it. It could be a private detective or no cop at all. Just go and talk to her. Let me know what you find out."

"Will do, sir."

Brand drove to the address on Benton Drive. He radioed the patrol post he'd be out of his car following up on the complaint. While he walked up the stairs, he tried to figure out what kind of apartment building he was in.

Brand knocked on the door of Apartment D. A woman opened the door. Her apartment was dark except for the dim light behind her. He could easily see she wore a pink, see-through negligee.

"Ruby West?" asked Brand. He suddenly feared this was some kind of setup. He couldn't organize his thoughts.

"Come in." She smiled and stepped back.

"I'm sorry. I can't come in. I'm here to investigate the complaint you filed with the highway patrol concerning the individual who approached you in the East Side Foods parking lot."

Her telephone rang. "Are you Trooper Brand?" she asked.

"Yes, ma'am."

He hoped it was the highway patrol on the phone. He hoped they had an assignment for him, that he could leave.

"They want you to radio the patrol post."

Escape! "Thank you, ma'am. We'll be in contact with you regarding your complaint." Brand quickly walked to his squad car.

"Copied, be en route," radioed Brand to the dispatcher.

After completing the assignment, Brand telephoned Lakes to tell him about Ruby West. Ron said they could talk after midnight when their tours of duty ended. He told Brand not to go back to her apartment.

Brand waited for Ron at the patrol post, but Trooper Jonsen spied Brand and came over. "Hey, Billy," he said with a wide grin, "I see this case on the log. You follow up on it?"

"Yeah, somewhat."

"Somewhat? What in the hell's that supposed to mean?"

"Got called away on another assignment down south. Never even got to ask her about her complaint. Glad, too."

"Why the hell would you be glad?"

Jonsen sat at a desk and turned his back to Brand. He looked through papers and chewed on a cigar. Neither

Jonsen nor Brand saw Lakes come in, lean against the doorway, and listen.

"The woman . . . I couldn't figure her out. She was alone and strange. Ron told me never to get in a situation where I was alone with a woman in her house with no one else with her . . . especially one like her."

"She built, Billy?" Jonsen asked. He didn't look up.

He continued to shuffle papers and chew his cigar. He rolled the cigar between his teeth. Brand wasn't sure he was looking for anything in the papers.

"Don't know," said Brand.

Brand saw Ron leaning against the doorway. He tipped his head in Jonsen's direction, and Lakes gave a bit of a nod.

"Hey, tell ya what," Jonsen said without looking up. "I'll handle it for ya, you bein' new and all. That'll put your mind at rest, won't it, *Bill*?"

Brand looked at Ron, who gave a shrug to let Jonsen have the case.

"Yeah, sure. Go ahead and take it. I'll sign it over to you right now. Okay?" said Brand.

"You do that, Bill." Jonsen said without looking at Brand.

Brand turned to Lakes. "There's no problem doing that, is there, Ron? George said he'd handle the lady with the mouth breather phone calls for me."

"Okay," said Ron. "I'll see it gets recorded that way."

Jonsen snapped his head around, then went back to shuffling papers. Ron and Brand completed their paper work. Jonsen left the post to go on patrol.

"Do ya know why Jonsen wanted that case, Bill?"

"It was real nice thing for him to do, Ron," Brand said. "He's been on my case since I got here. Maybe now he and I can get along better. Maybe he wants to turn over a new leaf. This is the first time he called me Bill and not Billy or Billy Boy."

"You know he's got a wife and two kids," said Lakes.

"I know he's married. What's that got to do with this?"

"Under the circumstances you did the right thing."

"What do you mean, Ron ... under the circumstances?"

"Just let it go. We may never hear another thing about it."

"How long has Jonsen been here?" asked Brand.

"Came about a month before you got here ... on a penalty transfer. He got caught messing with a woman he first met in line of duty when he was stationed down in District Three."

"Maybe I should tell him about the pink negligee. That woman came to the door in next to nothing, and what she did wear I could see through."

Lakes pointed his finger in Brand's face and said, "Don't you tell him! You let it go! I mean it, Bill. Keep your mouth shut! *You say nothin' about this to anyone. You hear me!"*

Brand nodded and said, "Yes, sir."

Lakes turned and walked away.

* * *

"Yeah, had this geezer in my squad while filling out the report," Ruzan was telling Brand. "I finished and watched him walk in front of my car on the way back to his. Right then and there, he fell over like a board. I called for an ambulance. He'd had a heart attack," Ruzan said to Brand.

"Hey, that was an excellent opportunity for mouth-to-mouth resuscitation and external heart massage. How'd that go?"

Ruzan gave him a horrified look. "My god, that old bastard was foaming at the mouth! I wasn't about to get my face close to that."

After Ruzan left, Brand stayed in the room a moment, trying to comprehend what Ruzan had said. *He's certainly aware*, thought Brand, *that resuscitubes are in the trunks of every patrol car.* Since the Highway Patrol was often the first vehicle on the scene, often ahead of any ambulance or tow truck, troopers were charged to keep airways open, but also to keep from touching the victim's face and mouth. They had equipment to help them with that sort of thing. Brand hoped he'd be presented with an opportunity someday to use the equipment in the trunk. He asked himself if Ruzan and Jonsen had been good troopers once, and something had changed them, or if they just slipped through the academy and their probationary periods without really making the necessary commitment to help the public.

The following day as Brand began his tour of duty, he thought about Ruzan's comments about the heart attack victim foaming at the mouth. Ruzan had not helped this man, so how had he fared? Had he lived? By now Brand was aware of the questionable behaviors on the part of police officers with other departments, but most of them had far less rigorous training and nothing as military as the State Troopers. While he hated to see any person in authority exibiting behaviors that harmed the public, he had greater difficulty resolving those behaviors in relation to troopers.

Brand decided to take a shortcut to his assigned patrol area. He drove down a side street, thinking about the virtues, or the lack of them, in some police officers, when a truck speedily backed in front of his patrol car and stopped at the loading dock. Brand approached the driver.

"Good afternoon, sir. May I see your driver's license, please?"

"What for?" the man said, irritated.

"Your driver's license, please."

The driver began to comply with his request. He stared at Brand, while he reached into his hip pocket and pulled out his billfold. He shoved it at Brand's face.

"Take your driver's license from your billfold, please."

"Hey, ain't got no driver's license. I got a chauffeur's license! And I ain't got no registration in my billfold, neither. It's in the truck."

The driver handed Brand his chauffeur's license.

"Mr. Clark, you were stopped for failing to yield the right of way. You backed your delivery truck across this street without first lookin' for oncoming traffic. You backed directly in front of me. If I hadn't slammed on my brakes, I would've hit your truck."

Clark wasn't listening. He reached into the truck and pulled out the registration from a plastic pouch. "Here's the registration!"

"Mr. Clark, you'll be required to appear in court for failing to yield the right of way. Court is Monday, Wednesday, and Friday at ten and one. What day and time would you like to appear?"

"What! You can't ticket me!" He pointed to the lettering on the side of the truck. "You can't give me a ticket. I'm on official business."

Brand was thankful the truck was parked at the ramp. He wasn't sure of the procedure for towing a delivery truck if the driver had to be arrested and post an appearance bond. This particular instance hadn't been covered at the academy. Maybe he should have just kept on driving, but it was too late now. He'd already told Clark he'd be ticketed.

"Mr. Clark, either you decide a day and time, or I'll put it at Wednesday at ten o'clock."

Clark stared at Brand. Brand stared at Clark.

Finally the man backed down. "Fine. Put it at one, next Friday." Brand handed Clark the traffic citation and drove to his patrol area. During his tour of duty, he thought about his promise to Loretta that he'd drive her and Catherine to visit her parents.

* * *

On his days off, Brand drove Loretta and her daughter south of the city to visit her parents. The winding rural roads contrasted sharply with the massive interstate highway system. The roadway had chuck holes and went from cracked asphalt, to gravel, to dirt. The heat didn't affect Loretta, her child, or Brand because her large Buick was air conditioned. Her husband had been making monthly payments on the Buick. She told Brand his life insurance paid off *her* car and *her* house.

"You'll be making a right just around the next bend, Bill. It's a sharp turn. Be careful."

Brand was well aware he should be careful.

After the turn, the Buick crawled up a narrow, winding road. Periodic shoots of grass grew through the middle of the two dirt tracks. He slowed and eased the Buick over the "washboard" surface.

"Does the township ever put a road grader on this?"

"Springtime, when the dirt's soft. They live only about a mile from here."

Brand thought about what he was doing. He looked briefly at Catherine sitting between them. He questioned why he'd want to get involved in such a situation. *Loretta's a widow. She has a child. I'm only twenty-one. What added responsibilities am I in for? Why am I going to see her family? Why would a man want to spend his time and money raising another man's kid? Am I just feeling sorry for her and her daughter because she was my first death notification? She wants a man to help raise her daughter, but it's her daughter, not our daughter. But Loretta's so beautiful, so kind, and such a good mother. Dad told me never to marry a widow because I'd always be competing with a ghost. Thank god I haven't touched her, let alone slept with her.*

"You'll turn right at the top of this hill then down a long lane."

Her maturity for her age, her beauty, and her accent were things he liked. He thought the refinement her automobile signified didn't belong in this environment. It was not meant to traverse bumps, hollows, and steep grades. He looked at Loretta. He thought her profound beauty also didn't belong in this environment.

Brand brought the car almost to a stop. He eased it over exposed rocks and around dips. He was concerned about damaging the alignment and the muffler. He didn't want to damage her car. He wondered if his being in Loretta's life would damage her . . . or him. His thoughts returned to the guest lecturer at the academy.

"Gentlemen, several months after the death of an officer, wives of other troopers usually will encourage the widow to begin dating. One often-heard comment from the wives is to say to the widow, 'children are an extra advantage in finding a good man.' Gentlemen, I want to go on record and advise you that this statement is a bunch of bull! Why? The reason why a police officer shouldn't marry a widow with a child is it's tough enough already for a police officer to make a marriage work. The last thing he needs is the responsibility of a ready-made family."

When they stopped and got out, Loretta said, "Be careful of this mud here, Bill."

Brand stepped over the muddy patch. A smell assaulted him—the stench from an open drain.

At the house, they found a woman sitting on a rocker on the porch. "Ma'am, please meet Bill. Bill, this my ma'am," said Loretta.

"Pleased to meet you, Mrs. Scofield."

With closed lips, the older woman smiled.

She's so thin, thought Brand. Her faded house dress hung on her.

She barely moved her lips and partially covered her mouth when she talked. Her teeth were stained, and black cavities crowded her gums. Her breath was strong.

Loretta asked, "Where's Pap?"

"They'un cuttin' wood," said Loretta's mother.

Loretta told Brand they cut their own firewood for cooking and heating.

"They'un a-comin'," said Mrs. Scofield, motioning through the small house to the rusted back screen door.

Brand looked through the rusted screen door. Catherine ran to her grandfather who was down the muddy path. The slightly built and bearded man strained pushing the wheelbarrow, loaded with firewood, up the hill to the house. A small boy pulled on one end of the rope tied to the front of the wheelbarrow, trying to help him. Another rope lay on top of the cut logs. Catherine grabbed the other rope and pulled. The man's face tightened with determination. He leaned hard into the wheelbarrow.

Brand walked out the screen door. He was careful not to let it slam. He rushed down the hill and got between the children, put a rope over each of his shoulders, and leaned into the hill. The children let go of the ropes. Before the children got to the house, the wheelbarrow was at the kitchen door. The man said nothing, just nodded. A tobacco juice stain tracked down his gray beard.

Loretta said, "Pappy, please meet Bill. Bill, my pappy, Gene."

"Pleased ameet ya." The man shoved out his hand.

"Glad to meet you, too, Mr. Scofield," Brand felt his strong grip.

"How long kin ya stay?"

Loretta said, "Leaving tomorrow. Bill's gotta be back for duty day after that." She smiled. She looked at Brand.

"What? Ya in the army?"

"Naw, he's a State Trooper, Pappy. He's an honest-to-goodness real trooper, Pappy." She smiled at Brand.

"No kiddin'? State Trooper! Be damned!" He shook his head in disbelief.

Loretta just smiled.

Brand remembered stories told at the academy about old men and young boys, who lived deep in the rural countryside, standing at attention and saluting when a state trooper drove by. Brand liked Loretta's mother and father. Gene and Brand spent the evening listening to the radio in the front room while Loretta and her mother talked in the kitchen.

*　　*　　*

The log read: *Ruby West of Benton Drive telephoned and spoke with the post commander in reference to a trooper named Jonsen contacting her. She said the officer took the information regarding the car title. Complainant accused Trooper Jonsen of making sexual advances. Case referred to District Headquarters for investigation.*

"Hey, what's this all about?" asked Brand. He wasn't as confused as he appeared, but he wanted to get Ruzan to tell him what happened to Jonsen.

"Well, it was your case first. What'd you think happened?" asked Jonsen, coming in just at that moment, looking thunderstruck.

Brand hadn't seen Jonsen before he asked his question.

"All I know is after I got to her apartment door, things didn't look right. Just didn't feel right," said Brand. "I was glad to have to leave for another call."

"Brand, you're so damn stupid. What the hell happened?" asked Jonsen.

"Nothin' happened. I didn't go in her apartment. Got called on an assignment, like I said. Then I came back to the post and mentioned her to you. Ron was here. You offered to take the case for me."

"That's it?" asked Jonsen.

"That's it, except I told her either I or another trooper would contact her about her complaint."

Jonsen turned from Brand. He walked to his squad car.

"What'd you do?" asked Ruzan.

"Nothin'... just signed it over to him. How was I supposed to know he couldn't control himself?"

"Guess ya know now, don't ya, you stupid sonofabitch. For whatever good it'll do him."

"Whatya mean?"

"Hell, he'll be transferred so quick it'll make your head swim, probably out west this time," said Ruzan.

"Isn't his wife goin' get tired of this? It's a wonder she hasn't divorced him long ago!"

"You're a prick, Brand! You knew all along he can't pass up a free piece of ass. Cops stick together. We're brothers! Just why should his wife leave him?"

"Screwin' around, that's why! My god, he's a married man!"

"Listen, you idiot . . . some women are just waitin' for us. Hell, one time a couple years ago I walked up to this car and was goin' to write a ticket for a stop-sign violation. No sooner had I stopped her and told her what I was goin' to do, she started to unbutton her blouse."

"Who ya tryin' to kid?" said Brand. "I may be a rookie, but I'm not so naive to believe that!"

"Well, it happened."

"Okay, what'd you do?"

"Well, whatya think? I acted like I didn't notice."

"What happened then?"

"You'll keep it quiet?"

"Yeah, sure, just tell me. All I ever hear is people tellin' me police officers get themselves in trouble with women. Nobody ever says who, what, when, where or why. I'm not sure what to believe anymore."

Brand wondered about honor among police officers. No matter what Ruzan told him, he knew he'd better keep it to himself.

"She continued to unbutton her blouse. She put both hands around her back, unsnapped her bra and said, 'Officer, you don't really want to give me that ticket, do you?'"

"What'd you say?"

"Said, 'Why not?'"

"She said, 'This is why not.' She dropped her bra into her lap. Man, she was built like a brick shithouse. No way she'd flunk the pencil test!"

Brand wondered what the pencil test was, but he figured he'd better not ask. He'd just get called stupid again.

"What'd you do?"

"Man, didn't do nothin'. She reached up and—"

"What about traffic?"

"Wasn't any traffic, you idiot. Ya think I'm a stupid sex maniac?"

Brand said nothing.

"That's an example. It doesn't happen often, but it happens. Listen, sometime when we're off duty, we'll get together. I'll show you the ropes to pick up broads."

Brand said nothing. He knew Ruzan was married.

*   *   *

"Car 833, Post 93 to 833."

"Car 833 to Post 93. I'm south of the post about two miles. Go ahead."

"Return to Post. Lieutenant wants to see you."

He wiped his sweaty hands on his trousers. He thought, *Shit! The lieutenant knows about Loretta. Damn, I've had it. He won't transfer me. He'll fire me because I'm still in my probationary period.*

He arrived at the post and presented himself to the lieutenant. "Sir, Trooper Brand reporting as requested, sir."

"Hello, Bill, how's it goin'?"

"Fine, sir, just fine."

"I called ya in to go over this complaint that was filed against you."

"Complaint, sir?"

His heart sank. Brand knew he should say very little—just enough to be polite.

"Yeah, but it's already cleared," said the lieutenant.

The lieutenant told Brand the local delivery employee he cited to traffic court five days earlier had filed a complaint with General Headquarters. The complaint stated that Brand was firm to the point of being overbearing and abusive. His manager also forwarded a complaint that Brand had interfered with their deliveries.

"Sir, that isn't true!" Brand's voice was quivering.

"The driver of the truck backed directly in front of me. I had to slam on the brakes. When I asked to see his license and registration, he became resistive, bordering belligerent. He asked me what right I had to interfere with his deliveries. This followed by my getting his chauffeur's license and registration. I then cited him to court for the violation. But I didn't interfere with the delivery. He'd already backed to the unloading dock before I approached him."

"Yeah, we know. Yesterday afternoon, the superintendent from their regional headquarters office telephoned. He got the true story from the driver. Both the driver and the district office manager who forwarded the complaints are going to be disciplined."

"Where the case stand now?" asked Brand.

"Closed. The regional director said he's pleased the Highway Patrol is a professional organization, and that it didn't show favoritism."

*   *   *

"Good afternoon, sir. You were stopped for a routine safety equipment check. May I see your driver's license and registration, please?"

Brand decided he'd set a goal to write ten repair slips for equipment defects during each tour of duty.

"Thank you, sir. Mr. Novak, would you turn on your headlights, please."

"Car 833, Post 93 to Car 833," the outside loudspeaker crackled, "Car 833, Post 93 to Car 833."

Brand knew by the dispatcher's voice something important was happening. He quickly ran back to the patrol car, flicked the switch for the inside speaker, and answered the dispatcher.

"Car 833 to Post 93. I'm on a traffic check at Symmes and Riverview. Go ahead."

"Be advised: two armed bank robbers are attempting to escape on foot near the Riverview Police Station."

"Copy. En route."

Brand ran up to the motorist's car and handed back the driver's license and registration. He told him he had a defective taillight, but there was no time to write him a repair slip.

Brand drove at emergency speeds to the Riverview Police Department.

"Post 93, Car 833 to Post 93. Be advised: I'll be out of service at the Riverview Police Station."

Brand grabbed the shotgun and six twelve-gauge double-ought buckshot shells from the glove box. He double checked to be certain the doors to the patrol car were locked. He'd heard stories about troopers who failed to lock their doors and wound up with their car either being stolen or the high-powered rifle or shot-gun in the squad car being used against them.

A Riverview police officer told Brand eight months ago the Riverview Bank had been robbed. The sub-jects were identified, and arrest warrants were issued. Twenty minutes before Brand arrived at the scene, one of the subjects went into a barber shop about a block from the police station for a haircut. The other subject waited outside. A police officer was in the shop getting his hair cut. When the barber removed the cloak from the police officer, the suspect panicked and bolted from the shop. Both suspects ran. The police officer chased the subjects on foot, but stopped when they fired two shots at him.

"What in God's name possessed these fellows to come back?" Brand asked the police officer.

"They're cocky sonsabitches," the officer said. "Probably drunk or high. They're hiding in the weeds over in that field. All we gotta do is to go in and get 'em," said the officer, pointing.

The officer finished telling Brand what happened when two carloads of deputies rolled up. Brand knew that, since he was the only state trooper, he wouldn't be taking a command role. The deputies wouldn't allow that, and they had the greatest presence at the scene.

The deputy in charge, a major, was the highest ranking officer. He ordered the officers to "fan out," to go into the field and to get those "bastards." The men obeyed. Brand knew many police officers and deputies had been in the military and would follow orders.

Two village police officers, twelve deputies, and Brand entered the field. The major ordered the officers to form a circle. Brand was trained at the academy on the rule of the triangle. *The logic for that is clear*, he thought. *You'd think the major would know it.* He worked his way over to the major.

"Sir, don't you think you ought to give the command for the officers not to fire towards the center?"

"Why the hell not? Those two bastards fired at one of us. We're gonna get their asses." He shook his shotgun in the direction of where the suspects were last seen.

"Yes, but we're in a circle. We'll be in the line of fire."

"Get back in the circle, statie, or clear out. You ain't one of us!" Brand backed off and went back to his position. The circle became smaller.

"There they go!" yelled an officer further across the field. Two loud reports from a twelve-gauge riot gun followed quickly after his shout. Brand saw a deputy running to cut off the fleeing felons' line of escape. The suspects were facing a winded deputy who had a shotgun pointed directly at the shorter man's chest. Brand expected both subjects to die instantly from double-ought buck tearing through their bodies.

"Stop, you bastards, or I'll blow your damn heads off!" said the deputy.

The circle rapidly closed on the suspects. Brand looked at the officers in the circle. He knew they wanted the suspects to run so they could take shots at them. The situation reminded him of when he was a boy and hunted deer with men. Brand thought, *To the deputies, there's no difference.*

"On the ground, and spread your arms and legs, you sonsabitches," commanded the major as he entered the circle.

The suspects fell to the ground and spread their arms and legs.

"John, watch this one," was his next command.

The major walked up to the prone suspects. He took the end of his shotgun barrel and rammed it in the nape of the neck of the terrified man.

"You make one move, you sonofabitch, and I'll blow your goddamn head off," said the major.

The suspects froze.

"John, search the one you got," said the major.

He was quickly searched. No weapon. The major ordered the other suspect to get up. He obeyed. The major removed his outer jacket. Several of the deputies yelled, "There it is! There it is!" But there was no weapon. His shoulder holster was empty.

"Hell, they must've tossed the gun. Where's it, you bastards?"

The suspects said nothing.

Brand, in a polite tone, perhaps too polite, asked the major if he was going to advise the suspects of their rights before he continued questioning them.

"Hell, they ain't got no rights. They lost 'em when they shot at one of us. Ain't that right, boys? Besides they already know their rights, don't ya, ya bastards? And besides that, shut your goddamn mouth, statie."

The major looked at Brand's nameplate above his badge and said, "Brand. I'll remember you!"

Brand said nothing. The major ordered several of the men to search the field for the handgun.

Brand walked back to his patrol car. He radioed the post that the subjects had been apprehended and he was returning to routine patrol. At four o'clock, Brand returned to the station. He wanted to talk with Lakes concerning the complaint against Jonsen.

Lakes told Brand that Ruby recorded both his and Jonsen's conversations.

"The lieutenant said there's no problem with what you said and did. He laughed and said you sounded nervous and scared," said Lakes.

Brand held up a hand as if being sworn in. "I plead guilty on both counts, Ron. I was nervous, and I was scared."

*   *   *

"Car 833, Post 93 to Car 833."

"Car 833 to Post 93, go ahead."

"Be advised of a possible fatality on the interstate at Code D."

Fifteen minutes remained before his tour of duty ended at midnight. But he had been called, so he responded. "En route to the possible fatal."

Brand wanted to begin the three-hour drive to Mandy's apartment immediately after his tour of duty ended at midnight. She had sent him a note. It read, *Bill, I've spent hours thinking about you. I'm waiting. Mandy.*

Now, it would be later, maybe much later. He drove toward the accident scene. A radio call advised him another trooper, one not assigned to his post, had been traveling through the county and came upon the accident. The accident was a head-on collision. A car had been traveling the wrong way on the interstate.

Brand radioed the dispatcher that he'd be out of his squad car at the accident.

Kneeling on the pavement, with his head and shoulders wedged inside the wreckage, Brand saw the unfamiliar trooper. His Stetson lay on the back seat. Brand saw his head rise a couple inches every few seconds. Brand leaned in and looked over the trooper's shoulder. He saw a small girl with golden hair. She was lying on the backseat floor. Her right arm was by her side. Her left arm was on the floor. Her hand, above her head, angled upward. She was about five years old. The trooper was giving her mouth-to-mouth resuscitation.

"She's breathing," the trooper said as he looked up at Brand. "Let's get her outta here. Use the blanket!"

Brand didn't know the trooper, but he felt his command presence.

Brand climbed over the seat into the wreckage. Each breath the little girl took made a gurgled, raspy sound. Brand looked at her face. Her right eyelid was closed. Her left eye was partially open. She seemed to be looking but not seeing from her blue left eye. Her face glowed in the night.

They eased the blanket under her body. Brand cradled her head in his hands. She struggled for each shallow breath. The expansion and contraction of her chest was all that moved.

Congested traffic prevented the ambulance from getting close to the scene. The trooper and Brand carried her across the median and onto the berm. They walked toward the ambulance. The trooper held the blanket supporting her body. Brand cradled her head as if he were an altar boy carrying holy water. Her golden hair was soft and fine. It flowed between his fingers. He felt her skull move under her skin, and it felt as if he had a bag of precious jewels cradled in his hands.

They carried her beside a Greyhound bus stopped in traffic. Brand looked up at the passengers. Red lights from the two squad cars swept over the bus windows. Passengers' faces pressed against the windows. They looked down on the child, on the trooper, and on Brand.

The ambulance took the girl.

Brand saw the driver of the crashed car leaning against the car the semi-tractor and trailer had ripped open. He cried. Over and over he said, "My baby, my baby . . . I killed my baby!" The smell of liquor exuded from him.

The truck driver explained he had been traveling east on the interstate and had pulled out to pass another semi-tractor and trailer. When he was almost past the rig, he saw a car coming straight at him. The oncoming car swerved, but the trucker had no where to go. He hit the car behind the driver's door.

"How's the little girl?" asked the truck driver. "I opened that car like a can of sardines."

Brand drove to the hospital to finish the accident report. He met the father outside the emergency room. Three hours had passed since the accident before Brand's had his first chance to question the father. He'd sobered up. He'd talked to a lawyer. The father said his attorney advised him not to talk to police. Brand walked to the emergency room. They were preparing the child for brain surgery. The surgeon told Brand there was little hope for the girl. She had massive skull fractures. Brand left the emergency room. There was more moisture in Brand's eyes than in the eyes of the father.

"Sir, you'll have to appear in court for driving the wrong way on the interstate. Court is Monday, Wednesday, and Friday at ten and one. What day and time next week would you like to appear?"

"Set any time ya want. My attorney said he'll handle it."

Brand set the court for Monday at ten. If the girl died, a charge of manslaughter could be issued by the prosecutor's office. Brand knew the possibility of a vehicular-manslaughter conviction was debatable. He'd learned in the academy when a family member was killed, juries were hesitant to convict the driver. They felt the driver had suffered enough because a family member had been killed. While driving from the hospital to the patrol post, Brand thought of a Carl Sandburg poem he'd read in his freshman English class about a hearse horse snickering every time he took a lawyer's corpse to the graveyard.

Brand reached the patrol post at two in the morning. He was going off duty for two days. He didn't declare overtime.

He was tired. He had been on duty twelve hours. He knew he needed rest before he started driving to see Mandy. It would be mid-morning before he arrived at her apartment. By then, Brand knew, she'd be in class.

At 9:30 in the morning, he reached her apartment. He walked to the Registrar's Office in Eaton Hall to get her class schedule.

Her last class ended at 3:50 p.m. He had six hours to kill. He saw Professor Whitcombe close her Eaton Hall office door and walk down the hallway towards him. She saw Brand.

6

THE LUST

"CAN I CALL YOU TROOPER BRAND?"
Professor Whitcombe asked.

"How nice to see you, Professor Whitcombe," Brand said.

"Can I call you Trooper Brand?" she repeated.

"Yes," Brand said, feeling slightly embarrassed.

"Well, then, congratulations, Trooper Brand. You decide to come here in person to see me? I wrote on your final exam to call me when you finished training."

"I remember, but, technically, I'm still training. I'm in my probationary period."

"I don't teach today. I only came onto campus to get a research paper from my research assistant. Walk me home."

Brand now took orders from highway patrol supervisors, not from civilians. He was no wet-behind-the-ears college kid anymore. He might still be in his probation period, and he still was only twenty-one years old, but he was at ease being the person in charge. He looked at her authoritatively. "Is that a request or command, Professor Whitcombe?"

His tone of voice visibly startled her. She paused and looked at him a little differently. Then her smile returned, and she said, "Would you be so kind, Trooper Brand, to accompany me as I walk myself home?"

He said nothing. He turned and walked beside her.

"Why didn't you call me?"

"If you remember, ma'am, you asked me to call when I finished training. I haven't."

"That the real reason?"

"Why the third degree, Professor Whitcombe?"

"Does it seem like I'm grilling you?"

"Yes, actually it does, Professor Whitcombe."

He wasn't in uniform, but he was in state-trooper mode. He might be young but he was taller than she was and looked down at her the same way he looked down at a driver who challenged him. He could see she felt his dominance, his command presence. He had learned to tell when drivers had been put in the proper frame of mind.

"Please quit calling me Professor Whitcombe. I'm not your professor now. Perhaps you could call me Vicky . . . *no* . . . call me Victoria. Yes, I would prefer if you'd please call me Victoria."

Brand didn't say anything.

"Bill, do you remember our last meeting in my office?"

"Yes."

"Yes . . ." she prompted.

"Yes, Victoria, I remember our last meeting in your office. You didn't want me to quit school."

"What else do you remember about that meeting?"

"I remember you asking me if I were going to be in school that semester . . . if I still planned to take your class."

"What else?"

"You said quitting could become a habit. I remember you telling me not to be a quitter."

Victoria lived very close to campus. Already they had arrived at her house. She and Brand stepped up to her front porch. He towered over her. His training had added a lot of muscle that hadn't been part of his college self.

"What else do you remember, Bill?"

"Ask your question again, Victoria."

"What do you remember, Bill?"

She was in teacher mode, trying to regain authority in that role. Brand said, "Again, Victoria, ask your question!"

He moved close to her. Her back was against the wall. She didn't move. Her neck arched. She looked up at him.

"Ask your question again, Victoria!"

"What else do you remember, Bill?"

He looked down at her. "I remember your blonde hair. I remember the wide pupils in your stunning blue eyes. I remember your full, white blouse. I remember your slender leg. I remember your waist. Your shape. I remember your red skirt. That, Victoria Whitcombe, is what else I remember."

"You've changed, Bill. You left a boy. You're back a man!"

"I was a twenty-year-old kid when I left school. I'm much older now. I've seen and done in one year what most men never see or do in their lifetimes."

"That's great, Bill."

"Why is that great?"

"Now I'm not the older woman."

He half grinned. "That you're not, young lady!"

"Please come in."

He did, and she locked her door behind them.

"My feet are killing me," she said. "I need to get out of these heels."

He waited as she left him to go to another part of the house.

He stood at her sink and looked out her kitchen window at her manicured lawn, her stately, well-trimmed trees that bordered the campus lake. He watched a male mallard clasp and mount a female mallard. It was that time of year.

He heard her soft footsteps come down her hallway.

"Bill, please don't turn around. Please close your eyes," she whispered.

He heard her soft footsteps approach him. He felt her arms slide around his waist. He felt her breasts press against his back.

She released him.

"Bill, please keep your eyes closed and turn around."

He turned.

"Now open your eyes."

He looked down at her. Her feet were bare. He saw the red skirt, her thin waist, her breasts jutting against the fabric of her white blouse.

She looked up.

He moved a step closer to her and put his hands on her waist. He firmly moved his hands up her back. Then he pulled her against his body and pressed his face on the curve of her neck.

"I want . . ." he murmured.

"What you want, Bill?" Her voice was soft, husky.

He lifted her and sat her on her kitchen counter, then circled her body with his arms, pulling her against his body again. He cupped her breasts in his hands, feeling like he needed more, so much more. He thrust his face in her breasts.

She rested her hands on his shoulders and slowly pushed him back, her eyes filled with passion. She unbuttoned his shirt. With her hands against his skin, she eased her hands up his chest and over his shoulders. His shirt dropped to the floor.

He unbuttoned her blouse, and she shrugged out of it. Then he squeezed her. He pushed her back against the counter wall. "You're right, Victoria. I'm not a kid anymore."

"I want you, Bill."

He put his hands on her knees, under the fabric of the red skirt, sliding his right hand up along the inside of her thigh. His left hand moved to the small of her back.

She wrapped her arms around his neck.

Nearly panting at this point, Bill whispered, "All you have to do is to tell me to stop, and I will."

She put her lips to his ear. He could feel her warm breath.

"*Don't be a quitter, Bill,*" she whispered.

* * *

Victoria knew the nature of men as professors, the arrogance they quickly developed, the entitlement. The only man she had ever been intimate with, she discovered was also a mama's boy, who now ran to his dean as he used to run to his mother, seeking comfort and affirmation. He was a mama's boy who couldn't confront a colleague face to face, who survived nowhere but in the ivory tower of academia—in the world of books and class schedules and assumed authority. Because he was man in age, and had treated her like fine crystal, she had assumed he was the kind of man she needed. But no. He had been soft, unconvincing, a man who talked like a man only. In the end, he disgusted her. She hungered for her *alpha* male.

"Take what's yours, Bill!"

They were animalistic, forceful. Together, Victoria and this young man, they were sensuous in ways she had only dreamed, only read about in her secret stash of paperback romances.

Some time later, still damp from their passion, they lay on her kitchen floor looking at the ceiling. "Remember, Bill, the first day of class when I said we were animals? This is the first time I felt like one . . . what pleasure! The student teaches the professor."

"Wrong tense, Vicky . . . *taught*. I won't ever again be your student, and you'll never again be my professor."

"My greatest fear, Bill, *was* that I'd marry a languid and uxorious professor who was nothing but a dainty mama's boy wearing a man's skin. You're not that!"

*   *   *

Mandy walked from the classroom after her last session. She saw Brand and smiled. "You look different, Bill. How do you feel?"

He shrugged. "Sad. I had a bad accident yesterday to investigate. It involved a little girl. It affects troopers more when an accident involves a child. The doctor gave her little chance."

"Do you think you identified her as you might a future child of yours?"

"I don't know. When I was holding her head on the way to the ambulance, I thought of a little girl I'm getting to know."

"Who's she?"

Brand mentioned Loretta's little girl. How he felt sorry for her and for her mother. He spoke of how nervous he was when he told the mother her husband was dead. He told Mandy of driving them to Loretta's parents.

He somehow missed her shocked look.

*   *   *

Brand got his suitcase from his truck. Mandy unlocked the door to her apartment. She knew he was tired. She didn't question him when he said he wanted to take a shower and go to bed.

Mandy showered after him. After she toweled off, she didn't dress, but eased into bed, pressing her naked body close to him. She had done this many times in the past. She felt safe next to him as she fell asleep. When she woke, she thought about *the widow*. Something had changed with Bill Brand.

She pulled the cover from Brand's chest and began gently kissing him. He moved. She continued her gentle kisses and gentle motions until he roused enough to join her. Afterwards they slept again.

It was nearly noon when Mandy woke and eased from her bed. Eighteen hours had passed since she'd seen him after her class.

"Will you come here next Friday?"

"I could, but why?" he said. "Your letter said you've 'spent hours thinkin' about me.' Still it's been a long time since our weekends."

He had never questioned her before about how often she wanted to see him. In his eyes, she had been the only act in town. Bill had been the kind of boy who, even though they said they shouldn't be exclusive, was exactly that. She knew this about him. But now there was the widow and her daughter. Mandy knew she'd lost control of him. He was no longer devoted to her exclusively like he had been in the past.

She wanted no commitments when he was in college and when he was at the academy. But her own freedom had never meant his in her eyes. She had been able to manipulate any man. She always got what she wanted. With Bill, this was no longer true.

* * *

Now, thought Brand, *there is Loretta and Victoria*. He wondered if Loretta's daughter liked him. Maybe it was too soon after her father's death for her to attach to another man. He wondered if, to Loretta, he was the transitional man, the rebound guy. He wondered if Loretta would be open to him emotionally. He'd read that in some women, their emotional drives were intense after a divorce or a husband's death. Then there was Victoria. Was he just a stud to her. He thought about those things while he looked at Mandy's body.

He wondered how Loretta's body looked. Mandy knew how to use her body and so did Vicky. He wondered if Loretta knew how to use hers. He wondered if Loretta was seeing other men. She was tall and thin—more angular than softly rounded.

She wouldn't look like Mandy when naked. *When a woman has a child, there's no doubt she's known another man*, thought Brand, but with Mandy, he didn't know for sure. Had she been with other men when he hadn't heard from her for so long? His thoughts went back to how she so pleasantly awakened him.

Brand wanted to keep his options open. He didn't want to commit to Mandy because there was Loretta. He didn't want to commit to Loretta because there was . . . Victoria.

He wondered if Victoria and he were ships passing in the night, just a male animal and a female animal's brief encounter to satisfy their carnal thirst and then move on. Yesterday, Victoria was an animal in high heat. Was he only a male animal she used to satisfy herself?

After dinner, Mandy and Brand showered together. They made love and periodically slept until morning.

*   *   *

During his drive back to his apartment, he found his thought going mostly to Victoria. He knew nothing about her personal life. Was she seeing anyone? The male professors he knew were refined men, their personalities different from those of state troopers. Yet, as a professor herself, Brand knew Victoria liked to be in charge.

But Brand had changed. No longer a college boy, he figured she knew he wasn't a man she could command or push around. He knew Victoria was an alpha female, but he knew in the year since he'd been a student at college, he'd become an alpha male.

*   *   *

The log read, *Be advised: Jackie L. Lancaster, age five, died at 4:27 a.m. this date. The cause of death was complications arising from skull fractures sustained three days earlier in an automobile accident.*

"Sir, request permission to leave my patrol area for about an hour and a half today. I want to go to the courthouse and talk to the prosecutor about this accident. She should charge the father with vehicular manslaughter."

"You know what she'll say," said the lieutenant.

"Well, sir, I think I know, but I've an obligation to try. I could handle it by phone, but I want as many points as possible on my side. I want to look her in the eye, to see her personally. I want her to tell me face to face she won't do it. I owe it to that little girl."

The lieutenant's face softened. "Go ahead, Bill, just advise by radio and go on in."

"Thank you, sir."

While driving to his assigned patrol area, Brand thought about his time with the patrol. He was beginning his second year. He wasn't a rookie anymore.

"Pull over in the parking lot," radioed Lakes. "I wanna talk a minute."

He eased his patrol car beside Lakes's squad car, coming from the other direction so their driver's windows were next to each other.

Lakes said, "I wanna tell you what happened to Jonsen."

Brand already knew the man was gone. "Where'd they send him?"

"Post 21."

"That's 200 miles from here. When's he gotta report?" asked Brand.

"Already has, at eight this morning."

"His wife . . . she know why?" asked Brand.

Lakes shrugged. "Don't know. She's gotta be wise to him. They haven't got much money. This'll really set 'em back. She's probably just resigned herself that she and their kids can't survive financially without his paycheck, so she puts up with him."

"How come they punish his family like this, Ron? Jonsen's got the problem, not the family. According to what you've told me, this has happened before. What does uprooting him and his family really do. Why don't they get him some professional help?"

"Bill, it's the brass. They don't want this to go on the record. The only way they can fire him is through civil service. What an embarrassing mess that would be. They're transferring him so fast because they want him to quit, to resign voluntarily. Then there's no mess."

"Shoot straight with me. How widespread is this?"

For a moment, Lakes looked out his windshield. Then he met Brand's eyes. "It's out there, Bill. The patrol will eventually unionize, and when it does, supervisors will lose leverage that keeps Jonsen's issues off the books. Then things will change for the worse. It'd be a lot harder on the family if he was fired."

"Why does unionizing make such a difference?"

"The union would be obliged to protect weak troopers like Jonsen. Management'll have to negotiate penalty transfers into the union contract. I don't see that happening."

"How come?" asked Brand.

"In every organization, there are those who do and those who take. Our takers are Jonsen and Ruzan. They'll pay their union dues—just like all of us will—and the union will give them the cover they need. When we do those safety checks, you know what kind of view we get of some women. The reason some police officers stop women is just because they can. Maybe they think they'll get lucky."

"I figured as much. When you were my field-training officer, you told me not to stop a woman alone after dark unless it was a significant violation. That must've been your reason."

"It was. It just scares the heck out of most women to be stopped late at night. They aren't sure if it's a police officer or a rapist. And even when they know it's an officer, they're never sure what he's gonna do. They worry about the uniform being cover."

"The more I talk to people, Ron, the more I find we have the best reputation in the state. It isn't as ethical as I thought it would be when I was at the academy, but compared to other law enforcement departments, we're way ahead."

Lakes nodded. "Remember what I said, Bill. In every organization there'll always be those who do and those who take. When you accept that, you'll have more peace of mind. Our good reputation is why they're making it rough on Jonsen. A man with his proclivities doesn't belong in the patrol. They want him out. When the union comes in, he'll be protected just like all the other takers. One last thing, Bill." Lakes hesitated, some uncertainty on his face. Then he leaned toward Brand at the window. "Promise me you'll keep this to yourself. Don't speak about it, ask me, or anyone any questions about what I'm about to tell you. Okay?"

"Okay, I promise, Ron. What is it?"

"Ruby West is a call girl. The lieutenant loaned her the patrol's tape recorder."

Brand nodded. Brand understood that Ron wanted him to know that he was the pawn in the lieutenant's and Ron's plan to set up and trap Jonsen. He also gave some thought to the idea that he had been tested as well.

*   *   *

Brand chose a wide parking area for the safety checks that had a stop sign a hundred yards away he could watch. He stepped onto the roadway to stop his first car.

He'd written three warnings for minor equipment violations before he saw a car bust through the stop sign, but then the driver saw him and was forced to slow down for his traffic check. Brand motioned to the driver to pull over.

Brand walked toward the car, but the driver had already hopped out and quickly walked toward him.

"Whatycha pull me over for?" barked a short, well-dressed portly man in his fifties.

"Sir, you failed to stop for that stop sign," said Brand. He pointed to the sign.

The portly man jumped up and down and screamed, "Yes, I did! I did stop! Oh, yes, I did! Yes, I did!"

Brand noticed with each jump he cleared the ground by nearly two feet, pretty impressive for so heavy a man.

He bent his knees almost to the point his heels touched his butt each time he jumped.

"Sir, your driver's license and registration, please."

"Man, I stopped!" the red-faced driver shouted.

"Sir, your driver's license and registration, please. And please return to your automobile."

The driver, trying to stand as tall as possible, strutted to his car, got in, and slammed the door. He handed Brand his operator's license and registration.

"Mr. Smalley, do you still live at 2719 Maple Avenue?"

"Yes," the man replied harshly.

"Your occupation, sir?"

"I'm a professor."

"Where do you work and how long have you worked there?"

Brand was trying to decide if he was going to cite the man to court or arrest him. When the man didn't respond right away, Brand said again, "Mr. Smalley, your place of employment and length of time there?"

"It's none of your business, asshole. I don't have to tell you nothin'!"

Brand smiled.

"Whatcha smiling at, you piece of shit?"

"For the last time, Dr. Smalley, what's your place of employment, and what's the length of your time there?"

Perhaps the little man heard the steel in his voice. After a pause, the man said, "State University. Tenured full professor. Twenty-five years. Satisfied?"

Brand was surprised. His experience with well-educated people was that they didn't lose their poise. They might plead not guilty, but they didn't lose their composure. He knew he shouldn't issue him a citation. If he didn't show up for court—and Brand didn't think he would—he'd have to go to the courthouse, pick up the bench warrant, find him, arrest him, and take him in to post bond. It was a lot of extra work.

"Dr. Smalley, you're under arrest for the stop-sign violation. You'll now come with me to post bond."

The professor opened his mouth in surprise. "Why you pompous sonofabitch!"

"What wrecker service would you like to tow your car?"

"Man, you're serious!"

"Quite serious."

"Well, I'll be damned."

"Sir, choose a wrecker service, or I'll call the next available one."

Brand could almost see the man deflate. "I get my gas right around the bend," said Professor Smalley. "Can I drive there and park?"

"Okay, I'll follow. Just bear in mind if anything happens to your car, it's your responsibility."

Smalley drove to the gas station and parked his car. Almost meekly, he climbed into the squad car. Brand drove to the courthouse with him. The man didn't say a word. Brand offered no conversation either.

"Post 93, Car 833 to Post 93."

"Car 833, go ahead."

"Be out of service with a motorist for bond posting. I'll then be at prosecutor's office."

"Copied, Car 833."

The clerk of court wasn't available for Smalley to post bond. Brand took him to the county jail to wait for the clerk of court.

"How long I gotta wait for the next asshole?" said Smalley to the booking sergeant.

The sergeant mostly ignored him. "Up to the counter! Empty your pockets and take off your ring, watch, and belt! The clerk of court won't be in for an hour. It's his lunch break. Oh, yeah, count your money, too," said the booking sergeant.

"Listen, you can't do this to me. I'm no common criminal. I'm a professor." He didn't jump up and down when he spoke to the sergeant.

"Hey, trooper, ya sure this guy doesn't belong over in juvenile court?" the booking sergeant said to Brand. Then the sergeant leaned over the counter and said, "Listen, mister, doctor, professor or whatever the hell you wanna call yourself, don't screw with me! The reason you're here is your piss-poor attitude! Do what I tell you to do when I tell you to do it, or I'll tack a disorderly charge on ya," said the booking sergeant.

Smalley's jaw fell, then it snapped shut, and he glared at the booking sergeant.

"Oh, hell, lock him up till one o'clock," the booking sergeant said to the jailer. "Maybe that'll teach this pompous prick some manners. Then take 'im to the clerk's office to post bond."

The jailer took Smalley by the elbow and led him off to a holding cell.

Brand said, "Sergeant, you wouldn't believe that guy. He jumped two feet off the ground three different times and screamed that he hadn't run the stop sign."

"Yeah, I believe it. There're all kinds of assholes out there."

Brand walked to the prosecutor's office and talked with an assistant prosecutor. He went over the accident involving the little girl in detail. He explained how the father was confused and drove onto the exit ramp of the interstate highway, ending up going the wrong way. Brand also described how he showed little compassion for his daughter after he'd talked to his lawyer.

"Had he been drinkin'?" she asked.

"I believe so. I could smell booze on him at the accident site, but can't testify to it. This is one of those slippery situations. He said he hadn't. He said he was so shook up after the accident that he took several drinks from the bottle he had in his car, but only after the accident. Could smell the liquor. And he appeared under the influence. But, of course, I never saw him driving, so I can't testify he was driving under the influence before the accident."

"Didn't you test him?"

"Wouldn't have helped. Witnesses told me they saw him drinking after the accident before I got to the scene. The test would've meant nothing."

"You're right," she said. "Before the officer gets to the scene, if the driver takes a couple of swigs and makes sure witnesses see him take those swigs, then any alcohol test the officer would take can't be used as evidence of his driving under the influence. The level of alcohol in his system wouldn't reflect the amount he had in him when he was driving. Several years ago, you could've arrested him for public intoxication. Now, being drunk in public isn't a violation, police can't arrest a person for pulling that kinda stunt."

Then the assistant prosecutor said, "Sorry for the long discourse. Drunk drivers are scumbags. They really piss me off. The only thing that pisses me off more is when an off-duty cop drinks and drives. Those sonsabitches oughta be castrated. I'd castrate 'em myself if it were legal. Well, anyway, about this accident . . . you want me to prosecute him for manslaughter, right?"

Brand didn't hear her question. He was wondering what happened to her that made her so emotional about off-duty cops who drank and drove.

"Trooper, ya want me to prosecute him for manslaughter?"

Brand focused. "That's right."

"You think I can convict him?"

"Don't know. That's why I'm here . . . to find out."

"Well, trooper, you know the first thing he'll do is request a jury trial. Is he handsome?" she asked.

"Not ugly. Why?" asked Brand.

"Harder for juries to convict handsome guys and pretty women. He married?" she asked.

"Yes, yes, he's married. First wife died . . . the mother of the girl. I didn't see his second wife, though."

"Did he lawyer up before you got a chance to interview him?"

"Yes. But at the scene I heard him spontaneously say, 'I killed my baby. I killed my baby.'"

"Well, chances are his wife will come in and sit directly behind him at trial . . . she'll cry at the right times. His attorney will make sure of that. Even if she doesn't miss the child that much, she'll look awfully sad. Jury will see a man who has lost his first wife through death and now seen his child die. They'll think he's suffered enough."

"Then you don't think they'll convict," said Brand.

"Nope. Nine out of ten cases never make it to trial . . . not worth our time and expense."

"Well, I had to try."

"Sorry, trooper. If we had the staff, and the court had the time, we'd give it a shot . . . just to make it rough on the bastard."

It was half-past one. He went back to the clerk's office to see if Smalley had posted his bond. He was just finishing up.

"Dr. Smalley, I'm heading back out. Want a ride to your car?"

Smalley looked at Brand. After a moment of indecision, the professor said, "Yeah. Um, thanks."

In the squad car, Smalley said, "Why you make me go through all that?"

"Because of how you acted. I figured you'd never show if I would've given you a summons to appear in court. If you didn't appear, the judge would've signed the back of the affidavit, and it would then be a bench warrant. I would've had to go to the clerk's office and get it. I then would've had to find you, arrest you, and take you in for booking."

"Why did that bookin' sergeant put me in a cell for forty-five minutes?"

"Because of how you acted. He never would've done it if you'd been respectful."

"What would've he done if I'd been nice?"

"He would've asked you to have a seat in the room you were in."

"Then what?"

"Then at one o'clock, he would've asked a deputy to walk with you to the clerk's office."

"Then what?"

"You would've posted bond."

"Then what?"

"The deputy would've left you there. Then you would've called a friend or taxi to take you back to your car."

"So, why are you taking me back to my car?"

"Because I'm done with what I had to do, and I'm driving back to the area where your car is."

"You mean I went through all of this just because I pissed you off?"

"You didn't piss me off, Dr. Smalley. You went through this because your actions told me you weren't a good risk. I thought you might not appear in court. If you didn't appear, I would've had to go through a lot more work just to get to the same result."

"What happens now?"

"That depends on what you do. You can appear in court and plead guilty, not guilty, or no contest."

"What would happen if I don't show up?"

"Dr. Smalley, you should talk to a lawyer about that."

"Do most people who post bond show up for court?"

"It depends on what the charge is."

"You charged me with a stop-sign violation."

"Correct. If you're convicted, it's two points on your driving record."

"What happens most of the time in cases like mine you've had when a person doesn't show up for court?"

"Like I said before, you should talk with your lawyer."

Brand stopped beside Smalley's parked car.

Smalley opened the squad car's door.

"Dr. Smalley, you said you're a professor. May I ask what you teach?"

With a hint of embarrassment, Smalley said, "Human Relations. May I ask you a question, young man?"

"Yes."

"You said I didn't piss you off. Why didn't I?"

Brand wondered if he should tell him the truth—no one his equal would offend him, and no one beneath him could offend him. "It's just my nature, Dr. Smalley, not to take offense."

Professor Smalley gently closed the squad car's door and walked toward his car.

* * *

"How'd it go with the prosecutor?" asked the lieutenant.

"No luck, sir."

"Well, least you gave it your best shot. Speaking of shot, damn good shot you made at the basketball game."

"Just happened to be at the right place at the right time, sir. Lucky we won. Professional football players sure know how to play basketball. I was impressed."

"Yup. Command staff didn't think they'd be that good," said the lieutenant.

"You know what really surprised me," said Brand.

"Let's hear it."

"Their good-looking wives. They looked like movie stars and were dressed to the hilt, too."

"How'd you see 'em?"

"After the game, the charity put on a fancy dinner for both teams and their wives. Trooper's wives weren't happy once they saw the football players' wives."

"You know, Bill, hot-looking women like that wouldn't be their wives if it weren't for their husband's fame and money."

"I guess so, sir."

7

THE VAIN

LORETTA SURPRISED HIM when she asked, "You seein' someone other than me, Bill?"

"Where's Catherine?" asked Brand.

"She's spendin' the night at my sister's."

"Why you asking, Loretta? Are we supposed to be only seeing each other?"

She didn't answer. Her eyes told him she was waiting for a better answer.

"I have a friend. Name's Mandy. She does her thing. I do my thing."

"What's your thing, Bill?"

He didn't like her directness. He wondered what she was searching for. He decided he'd better take control. "May I ask you a question, Loretta?"

"Sure, Bill."

"You look so young, but you're so mature."

"That's not a question. That's an observation."

Brand looked at her. He was thankful she'd sent Catherine to her sister's house.

"You want me to tell you how old I am. After I tell ya, you're going to subtract five. Then you'll know my age when I had my Catherine. Then you'll know how old I was when I got myself pregnant. Anythin' else you wanna know? Do the math. You tell me. How old am I?"

"Twenty."

"Don't make me guess. How'd you know I'm twenty?"

"Didn't know for sure. Made an educated guess."

"Okay, now educate me."

"About a hundred miles separated us when we were young. You and I grew up the same way. We both lived way out of town and up a holler. Town folks called us 'woodsies,' and we called them 'townies.' Guys talked about girls. We could tell if they were of 'a bleedin' age.'"

"You know that and I know that. Tell me how you know I'm twenty?"

"Here's how I know. When I was a high-school freshman, my first girlfriend was in the seventh grade. No doubt she'd reached puberty. Older guy on bas-ketball team asked me if Lavonne and I were serious. Don't know why I said 'no,' but I did. I really liked her. He asked me if I minded if he asked her out. Don't know why I said, 'go ahead,' but I did. Guess I figured she wouldn't go out with him. He asked her out. Six months later Lavonne was pregnant, married, and four-teen. That, Loretta, is how I know you're twenty."

"You said we grew up the same way. What'd you mean?"

"You're a girl, maybe should've said in a similar way."

"How similar?"

"Far from town, dirt and gravel roads, mud or dust everywhere depending on the season, lucky if we got to town once a month."

"Tell me about your mom, dad, brothers, and sisters."

"Had a wonderful sister. She died. By the time the doctor got there, it was too late. No brothers, and I've the best mom and dad a boy could ask for. Dad died, though."

"How?"

"Emphysema . . . smoked too much."

"You said he was the best dad a boy could have. How so?"

"Dad had a hard life. Wanted me to do better than he did. Said he'd let me be a kid and play until my eighth birthday. Said to me, 'The day after you're eight years old, I'm gonna start workin' you hard. You'll hate to make your livin' as a laborer when you're a man. You'll get an education. You won't end up like me.'"

"What else he say?"

"He said, 'As long as you live in my house, put your feet under my table and eat my food, you will do what I tell ya to do. If ya don't like it, there's the door.' Said, 'If ya ever bring shame to the family, don't you worry what the police'll do to you. Worry about what I'll do to you when I get ya home.'"

"How'd you like that?"

"He had strict rules, but he told me in advance what the rules were. I knew exactly where I stood with him. I knew he said those things because he loved me. I loved pleasing my dad. He didn't want me to make the same mistakes he'd made."

"You didn't resent his taking your childhood?"

"He didn't take anything from me. I made work a game. I made it fun. I always worked alone. Gave me time to think, to dream."

"What else did he teach you?"

"Resilience. He taught me to be on time, to respect authority, to value education. Most importantly, he taught me to obey rules. I was named after my dad. He was called 'Big Bill.' I was called 'Little Bill.' Here's a way he taught me it's important to be on time. During the summer I turned sixteen, he said I could spend either Friday or Saturday evenings in town. I always picked Saturdays. He'd drop me off at a restaurant at six o'clock. Said he'd be back at eleven o'clock sharp. We'd synchronize our watches when he dropped me off. He said, 'If you aren't at the restaurant at eleven o'clock, I'll leave. You'll walk home.'"

Loretta grinned. "So, did he keep his word? Was he always there at eleven?"

"Sure was, but one time I wasn't. I was at my girl-friend's house. I looked at my watch, and it was five to eleven. Ran from her house. When I rounded the last corner before the restaurant, I saw dad's taillights as he drove away."

"What time was it then?"

"One minute after eleven."

"You hurt by that?"

"Nope. I just thought, that's my dad."

"What'd you do?"

"Walked home . . . got home at 1:45. Had a full moon. It was a nice walk. I figured if I had to walk home, I might as well enjoy it."

"What your dad do?"

"Waited up for me. Looked at me and said, 'Learn your lesson?' I said, 'Yes, sir'."

"And he left it at that?"

"He said, 'Get yourself to bed. You got work to do in the morning. Loretta, I feel like you're interviewing me!"

"I am. If ya loved your dad so much, how come ya quit college and basketball?"

"He was dead by then, but I asked mom."

"What'd your mom say?"

"She said, 'Billy do what you've gotta do, but promise me one thing. Promise me you'll finish college.'"

"Sounds wise . . . what'd you say?"

"I told her I would. So why are you interviewing me? We're just gettin' to know each other."

"I know, and I know after you hear what I have to say you may never come back."

"Go ahead, Loretta."

"I need to know the kinda man you are, not only for me, but for my Catherine. We come as a package. My first responsibility is to Catherine, and it'll always be that way until she's grown. Now, she just thinks of you as some guy who drove us to see her grandparents. Maybe that's all you are. I won't expose her or me to any man unless I know he's a good man, and that he's in it for the long haul."

"I see."

"I don't have fancy schoolin' like your Mandy has, but I'm wise to the world. I graduated from the school of hard knocks. I know what it's like to been married to a man who thought only of himself, who visited other women, who blamed me for gettin' pregnant and who saw me and Catherine as chains around his neck. No man will ever again lay a hand on me or my Catherine. If we continue to see each other, I'll have rules just like your dad had rules."

"What are your rules, Loretta?"

"When Catherine's near, there is no physical contact between you and me. I don't need a man in my life. It'd be wonderful to be married to a good man, but I'm not on the hunt for a husband. Carl's life insurance is enough to take care of Catherine and me, so I don't need a job. I can devote my time to raisin' Catherine the right way. You said I'm mature. I am. Your father made you grow up fast. I grew up fast, too. I'm goin' be blunt about the next rule."

"Go ahead, Loretta."

"Until I'm married there's no sex. Huggin' is fine. Holdin' hands is fine. So's kissin'. Everything else is off limits until I'm married. I'll be the perfect role model for my Catherine. I behaved like an animal only once, and I got myself pregnant. Never goin' to be an animal again. Animals don't marry. Human beings marry. Once a man and a woman marry, they ain't animals no more."

"I like knowing the rules, Loretta, and I like to follow them. I have a rule for you."

"Seems fair. What's yours?"

"My rule is we're friends and only friends until we agree to be in an exclusive relationship."

"What exclusive mean?"

"It means closed, barring all others. It means you'll date only me, and I'll date only you."

"Rules are rules, Bill. You abide my rule, and I'll abide yours."

* * *

Brand patrolled the interstate highway for the first part of his eight hour tour of duty. He paced a vehicle traveling eight miles above the posted speed limit. His practice was to allow seven miles over the limit. Seventy-eight miles per hour in a seventy-mile-per-hour zone merited a warning.

Before he left his squad car, he wrote the license-plate number of the stopped vehicle on a note pad.

He left the pad in the squad car. Brand learned this at the academy. If he were killed, chances were the killer wouldn't run back to see if he'd written down his license-plate number. With that, they could catch him.

"Good afternoon, sir, may I see your driver's license?"

"Certainly, officer, but it's in my briefcase on the back seat. Can I get it?"

"Yeah, sure, go ahead."

Brand replied without realizing what he was saying because he saw a clerical collar hanging on a wire hanger on the hook over the right rear window. He thought about the minister he'd arrested for indecent exposure. He wondered if he'd lost his church. He couldn't undo what he'd done, and what he did to Reverend Tanner was the worst thing he'd ever done in his life.

He saw the driver open his door, push forward the driver's seat, then reach for and open his briefcase. He saw him do these things, but he'd lost situational awareness because the clerical collar set him to thinking about the minister he'd arrested for indecent exposure.

He lifted his eyes from the driver's hands. A trooper should never do that. He saw that clerical collar hanging on the wire hanger and wondered if the driver was a minister. Then he wondered why a minister would hang his clerical collar in his car window so everyone could see it. Did he hope if he were stopped by a cop he'd catch a break or was hanging a clerical collar in a car's window an advertisement for homosexual men to see. He wondered if the driver really was a minister.

The driver pulled a black object from his briefcase, then quickly turned toward Brand. He thrust the black object to within six inches of Brand's stomach. Every muscle in Brand's body tightened. The driver had been so quick Brand saw only the black blur. His muscles froze. Air rushed from his lungs.

"Here it is," said the driver.

Brand slowly lowered his eyes. The black blur was a billfold. He took a breath and said, "Would . . . would you please take your driver's license and registration from your wallet?"

Brand was shocked that he allowed himself to be distracted. Never again. He knew he'd be dead if that black blur had been a gun.

"Thank you, sir. The reason I stopped you is that you were eight miles over the speed limit."

Brand advised him to stay within the speed limit. He didn't ask about the clerical collar because he didn't want to know.

Even after the man had driven off and Brand was back in his squad, he couldn't relax. At the academy, it had been drilled into cadets' brains never to let their guard down. During boxing week, he was knocked out because he'd let his guard down. *Today*, he thought, *I could've been killed because I let my guard down.*

He remembered Trooper Bice congratulating the cadets who returned to the Academy the Monday after boxing week. He said the commandant and command staff members weren't there to watch boxing. They were there to see which cadets had tenacity. To see if any cowards or shirkers remained. He said the purpose of boxing week was to weed out the last of the quitters and to determine where to station the cadets who graduated.

He remembered Bice saying there's another lesson to learn from boxing week. He said several of the cadets let their guard down and were knocked out. He said it was a good lesson to remember because "One of the times when you're a trooper, and you let your guard down, you won't be knocked out. You'll be dead."

He thought about the academy film where the officer was killed because he allowed the motorist to get out of the car and stand too close to his right side. While the officer was writing the ticket, the motorist pulled the sidearm from the officer's holster and emptied six rounds into the trooper.

Another training film had the trooper stop a beautiful blonde in a low-cut dress driving a convertible. While the officer walked up to her, he focused on her body and the smile she gave him. The trooper neglected to scan the back seat and floor of the car. A man crouched down on the floor of the back seat jumped up and put four rounds into the trooper.

Brand thought about the studies he'd read concerning the strength of thread used in making holsters that had to be strong enough so an assailant couldn't rip the revolver from the holster. *All this is of no value if I get myself killed because I let my guard down.*

Brand pulled his cruiser into a crossover median to watch traffic. He started to relax. He remembered an instructor saying, "If you're killed in the line of duty, you could've let your guard down. You could've made a fatal mistake."

Brand was still thinking about officers getting killed when a car sped by at a high speed. The driver backed off his speed when he saw Brand in his rearview mirror. Brand pulled him over.

"Mr. Tierman, you saw me in the crossover, didn't you?"

"Yeah, I saw you."

"Why did you still travel ten miles over the limit when I was following you?"

"Didn't know I was. Just got new tires. Speedometer must be off. Read sixty-eight miles per hour."

Brand checked his driver's license record with the dispatcher. He learned this violation, added to others, would mean license revocation.

"Mr. Tierman, you'll have to post bond for the violation."

"Please, officer, don't do this. It'll mean my license. I gotta use my car for work."

"Do you have a preference of a wrecker, Mr. Tierman? I won't allow you to drive to the bonding station because of your past violations. With this one, your driver's license will be revoked."

"Christ Jesus, man, ain't you got no feelings?"

"I got lots of feelings, Mr. Tierman. Chronic speeders are a danger to a lot more people than just themselves. I got feelings for those folks, too. And there's more of them than just you."

Brand arrested Tierman and had his car towed. His tour of duty ended.

* * *

Mandy phoned. She said she went to Mexico during spring break. She asked about Loretta and Catherine and asked if she could see him Friday.

"I'm scheduled to work this weekend, Mandy."

"Bill. *Please!*"

"Okay, Mandy. I'll put in for two days' vacation."

* * *

His alarm clock rang at ten o'clock in the evening. Brand stopped making the perfect academy-style bed. He stopped his one-hour-before-duty ritual of spit-shining his shoes, holster, and belt assembly. He now spent a few minutes each day with the polish.

The snow stopped falling when Brand reached his patrol area. He was working the south third of the county. He decided to check a large state park before driving the length of the interstate to look for disabled vehicles. He eased his patrol car along the snow-covered parkway. Tire tracks led from the parking area toward the lake. There was no road leading in that direction.

"Post 93, Car 833 to Post 93."

"Go ahead."

"I'm at the state park rest area about two miles in from Parkway. Got tire tracks leadin' off the parking area down toward the lake. Out-of-service. Investigating."

"Copy, Car 833."

"If ya don't hear from me within a half hour, send assistance."

"Copy, Car 833."

Brand parked and locked his squad car.

He walked beside the tire tracks. The light from the moon was bright. He didn't need his flashlight. He saw the automobile.

Brand remained motionless for several minutes. The only foot tracks in the snow were his. He knew there was at least one person in the vehicle, perhaps more. He didn't think anyone would drive into an area like this just to be alone with a woman . . . or a man. The chances of getting stuck was too great.

He crouched and looked through the back window. He saw nothing. He cautiously approached the automobile. He unsnapped his holster strap. He placed his hand on the butt of his revolver.

Brand looked into the car. He didn't turn on his flashlight. In the moonlight, he saw a person lying face down on the front seat. He saw no one on the back seat or floor.

Brand turned on his flashlight. The man's hands were under his stomach. Brand drew his revolver. He continued to watch him.

Brand opened the driver's door. He watched for some quick movement. A trooper from another post had been shot a month earlier in a similar situation.

"Highway Patrol, mister. Don't move an inch. That's the barrel of my gun you feel pressed against your head."

Except for opening his eyes, the man didn't move. If he brought out his hand from under his body and if that hand had a gun in it, Brand knew he'd pull his trigger. If the man were not killed instantly, Brand knew he'd surely die.

"Keep those hands under your body. Don't move them!"

The man complied.

"Now, your right hand, bring it out slowly. Don't move anything except that arm and hand."

The man's shoulders and head seemed to be forcing the seat downward. He made every effort to comply. The right hand eased slowly into view. No gun.

"Now, the left hand, bring it out. Do it slowly."

The man complied. No gun.

"Now, roll over on your side, toward the front of your car. Keep those hands where I can see them."

Brand saw no gun. He holstered his revolver.

"Now get out of the car. Do it slowly."

Brand stepped back fifteen feet from the vehicle. His right hand rested on the grip of his revolver. The man moved lethargically. He stood ten feet from Brand. His hands were raised. He said, "Nobody cares." With that he fell forward.

Brand took two steps backwards and let him fall. The man landed hard on his face and hands.

Brand watched him, then moved slowly toward the man lying face down in the snow. White snow turned to pink beside the man's left hand. Broken glass protruded through the snow. The man had cut his hand when he fell. Brand turned him over and directed the beam of his flashlight into his eyes. He was unconscious. Brand looked inside the automobile. On the dashboard he saw a bottle of gin two-thirds empty. Beside the gin was a prescription bottle containing three red-and-white capsules. Brand put the gin and prescription bottle in his coat pocket. He wrote down the vehicle's license number. He checked the man again. He was breathing and had stopped bleeding. After searching his outer clothing for weapons, Brand tried to lift him. He couldn't.

He pushed the man into a sitting position. From the back, he reached around under the man's arms, locked his hands, and dragged him to his squad car.

"Post 93, Car 833 to Post 93."

"Go ahead."

"I'm at the state park rest area about two miles inside the Parkway. I got a subject in the car. The man's about twenty-five years old and unconscious. I'm en route with him to Central Receiving Hospital. Break."

A dispatcher had asked Brand to start using BREAK because the dispatchers were getting behind typing long messages. He often had to repeat parts of the message. The periodic breaks gave the dispatcher time to catch up.

"Go ahead."

"Request you telephone Central Receiving. Advise them my ETA is twenty-five minutes. Advise them the subject is believed to have overdosed on some drug—red-and-white capsules plus a large amount of gin. Break."

A moment later the dispatcher said, "Go ahead."

"Send the next available wrecker to the Parkway two miles into the state park at the parking area. They'll see car tracks plus my footprints and the drag marks of a man. Advise them to tow the vehicle, a Ford sedan bearing local tags A 1642 Z. Run the registration. Over."

"Copy, Car 833."

"Car 833 out."

Brand turned the patrol car north. The unconscious man, secure in the seatbelt, flopped back, forth, and sideways.

"Car 833, Post 93 to Car 833."

"Car 833 to Post 93, go ahead."

"Got registration on A-Adam 1642 Z-Zebra. Can you copy?"

"Go ahead."

"Ford sedan registered to Michael David Proshenski, 1481 Lakeshore Drive."

"Copy. I'll be out of the car at Central Receiving."

Two orderlies were waiting. They got Proshenski onto a gurney and wheeled him to the emergency room.

"What happened?" asked the doctor.

"Found him parked along the lake down at the state park. He couldn't have been there long. Got him awake about forty-five minutes ago. Crawled out of his car. Said, 'Nobody cares' and fell face down in the snow. Cut his hand on some glass. Been unconscious since ... about forty minutes. Here's the gin, prescription bottle, and the three capsules that were on his dash."

He handed the nurse the capsules, pill container, and gin. He went outside and parked his squad car away from the emergency entrance. He went back inside.

"Please come with me," the nurse said to Brand.

He walked through the large, swinging doors. The doctor started guiding a tube up Proshenski's nose. He looked over at Brand and said, "Don't know how many capsules he took or how much he drank. Going to clean him out."

Proshenski thrashed his head, fighting the tube.

"Swallow, sir. Just swallow the tube," said the doctor.

A nurse handed Brand the driver's license. It read, *Michael David Proshenski, 1481 Lakeshore Drive.*

"That's enough information for me now. He'll be here tomorrow night? I'll need to talk to him to finish the report," said Brand.

"You'll need to sign the form so we can keep him here," said the doctor.

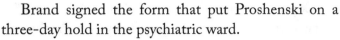

Brand signed the form that put Proshenski on a three-day hold in the psychiatric ward.

"Post 93, Car 833 to Post 93."

"Go ahead."

"Back in service, heading south to return to routine patrol."

"How's Proshenski?"

"He'll be there a while," said Brand.

8

THE FRAIL

"POST 93, CAR 833 to Post 93," radioed Brand.
"Post 93, Car 833. Go ahead."

"Two miles north of the county line on the interstate. It's snowing bad with twenty-mile-per-hour northwest wind. Got a weather report?"

"Post 93 to Car 833."

"Just over the wire: heavy snow, eight inches by midnight. Travel advisories all over this region."

Brand drove from the interstate to a gas station with a lift. The attendant raised his squad car. Brand released fifteen pounds of air from the rear tires, put on tire chains, and put the pressure back to thirty-two pounds. His chains were snug.

He backed out of the garage, drove to the gas pumps, and started topping off his tank.

"There's a car in the median about two miles down the interstate," said a man also getting fuel. He motioned south.

"Damage?" asked Brand.

The man, dressed in a light-colored trench coat and wearing no hat or overshoes, shook his head. "Didn't see any. Just looks like he lost it in the snow. It's gettin' bad."

"Yep . . . gonna be nasty," said Brand.

Brand bought two cheese sandwiches from the vending machine. He wanted coffee, but knew better. When tied up with accident after accident, there was no time to go to the restroom. His shift ended in an hour, but he suspected it'd be a long time before he'd be off duty.

"Post 93, Car 833 to Post 93."

"Go ahead."

"Motorist advised of a car in the median at about the county line. En route. Be there in five minutes."

"Unit 833, advise after you're finished. We've three more traffic accidents. No personal injuries reported."

"Will do. Car 833 out."

The driver had stayed with his car in the median. Brand walked over. "Hi, any damage to your car, sir?"

"Naw, just slid off the road. Damn, it's slippery," said the motorist.

"Sure is. You'll need a wrecker," said Brand.

Brand put his back to the wind to help block the snow.

"I'm a member of the Auto Club," said the driver.

"Take this for what it's worth, but Auto Club membership doesn't do much good in this kind of situation.

Their wreckers are the first called. May take six to eight hours to get one out here."

"Membership costs me fifty bucks a year. That's not very good service."

"Not their fault. Auto Club membership's fine in decent weather. Closest Auto Club wrecker is eight miles. There're two other wrecker companies, not Auto Club, within a few miles. Backed up on calls, too. Take 'em a couple of hours before they can get to you."

"Well, officer, do what you think is best."

"Sorry, you tell me. Just tell me quickly," said Brand.

Brand cupped his hands around his mouth and blew warm air over his face. His black coat and gray slacks were turning white.

"Call me one of them Auto Club wreckers. I'll wait."

"Okay, I'll need your membership card. You got blankets for you and your wife?"

"Got a couple in trunk." He handed Brand his Auto Club card.

"I'll radio it in. Be back in a few minutes."

When he returned to the stranded car, the driver had gotten out the blankets and was handing them in to his wife. "Here's your card. Dispatcher said it'll be over four hours. Keep your windows cracked when you run your engine or carbon monoxide will build up."

He walked back to his patrol car. Three inches of snow had fallen. Snow covered the highway. Traffic moved at twenty miles per hour. Brand brushed snow from his uniform and got back in his squad car. He wondered how many more hours the couple would be stranded.

The day filled with accidents stacked upon accidents. All cars from the patrol post were working with on- and off-duty troopers. Most were minor-damage accidents. At three o'clock in the afternoon, six inches of snow had accumulated. Brand was an hour late arriving to each accident. His next accident call was toward the county line near the location of the first stranded motorist he'd contacted shortly after daylight.

"Everything okay here?" Brand stopped to speak to the man and woman whose car was still in the median.

"Seen wreckers all day," said the driver. "None stopped. What's going on?"

"Auto Club wreckers work from a list that's first called first served. It's a long wait to get one durin' bad weather."

"Please officer, call me any wrecker. We've gotta get outta here."

"It'll still be awhile, probably a couple of hours. I got a cheese sandwich. Want it?"

He gave one of his cheese sandwiches to the couple. He radioed dispatch for any available wrecker. Brand eased his patrol car back into light traffic and drove toward the next accident.

* * *

He saw a man waving his arms. He eased his patrol car to the berm. It was impossible to judge the edge of the roadway. The only reference points were reflectors on metal poles that marked the edge of the berm. Brand opened his window.

"My wife," said the frantic man, "she's havin' a baby!" Tears ran down his face. His hands were red from the cold.

"Let's go!" Brand jumped from the patrol car. He walked and slid down the hill to the disabled car. When he arrived, he poked his head in the car and saw the woman sprawled in the passenger seat.

"What's the situation? The doctor she's seeing, did he mention any complications?" asked Brand.

Brand looked at the man. He'd been outside too long. He was shaking from the cold and blowing snow.

"Hey," he said sharply to get the man's attention. "Focus. Talk to me! Did the doctor say there'd be any complications?" Brand spoke forcibly directly in the man's face.

"No, no complications. He just said to get her to the hospital when the pains started."

Brand could barely understand him. He was shaking and crying.

"This her first child?"

He nodded.

The husband's hair and the front of his clothes were caked in white. When he moved, thin white crusts of cracked snow broke loose and swirled away.

"Get in your car and get warm. I can't do anything for your wife down here. The car's too much at an angle. Just go around and get back in your car."

The nearly frozen man moved. Brand opened the passenger door. "Hello, ma'am. Highway Patrol. How's goes it?"

"Got labor pains . . . bad!"

"How far apart?"

"One on top the other!"

She screamed. She drove back her head and shoulders. Brand closed the door.

He stood in the blizzard beside the car and closed his eyes. He knew what he had to do. He didn't feel the cold anymore. He thought, *My God, I'm going to have to deliver a baby!*

He opened the door.

"You gettin' any warmer?" he asked the husband.

The man nodded, still shaking but also dripping.

"Okay, stay put. I'll be back. We'll carry your wife up to the patrol car where it's level. Delivered a couple of babies, so there's no problem. Just stay here for now. Get warm. We don't want a frozen father now do we?"

Brand knew he should comfort the expectant mother. The best way to do this, he believed, was to show command presence. Brand hadn't actually delivered any babies, had never even seen a baby born. He'd read a chapter and had seen a short film on emergency childbirth in his first-aid class at the academy.

Brand grabbed her suitcase from the back seat.

"Try to relax. I'm going up to the patrol car. I'll be right back."

With her suitcase in one hand, Brand climbed his way up the hill. Snow swirled. He could barely see their vehicle from his squad car.

He got the first-aid kit, a rubber sheet, two white sheets, and two woolen blankets from the trunk. He turned the heater and blower to high. He reached for the microphone:

"Post 93, Car 833 to Post 93, Emergency!"

The dispatcher replied, "All units . . . no radio traffic. Go with your emergency traffic, Car 833."

"One mile north of county line on the interstate south bound. Going to be delivering a baby. No traffic on the interstate."

The lieutenant took the microphone from the dispatcher and said, "Copied your situation. It's not possible to send assistance. We closed the interstate about five minutes ago. Once all outbound traffic has cleared, I'll try to get a plow out to you."

"Car 833 to Post 93. Copy."

Brand unfolded the rubber sheet. He draped it over the back seat. He put the white sheet over the rubber sheet. He took from her suitcase everything that could be used to soak liquid.

He took the other blanket and slipped down the hill to the pregnant woman and frightened husband. Five minutes passed since he'd left them.

He opened the door and saw the husband dabbing sweat from her forehead with his handkerchief. Brand wrapped the blanket around the woman. She bolted forward with contractions.

"Help me get your wife up the hill."

The husband didn't move.

"Hey, mister, I need your help!"

The man still didn't move.

"Listen, don't you come up to the patrol car until you hear the siren. When you hear it, get up there fast."

The husband slowly nodded his head.

Brand took the woman into his arms. She was small. The blanket covered her. She moaned and screamed. Three times he fell to his knees as he forced himself up the hill.

Nearly out of breath Brand gently placed the woman on the back seat of his squad car. He told her the last birth he handled was right here in this very same back seat, and both mother and son were fine.

She wore white slacks. They were wet and pink. He didn't know how to tell her he had to remove them. He knew he had no time. She was incoherent. Brand was baffled.

"Just get 'em off me!" she screamed.

He pulled off her slacks and underpants.

He put her shoulders in the corner of the back seat, then put her right ankle on top of the back of the front seat. He draped her from the waist down with the sheet. Brand remembered that the sheet, according to the first-aid book, served the purpose of limiting the woman's embarrassment by making her think she was covered. He doubted the sheet had its intended effect, but it served the purpose of keeping her warmer. He covered the rest of her body with two blankets and tucked them under her shoulders. The blizzard howled.

Brand looked under the sheet, seeing the wrinkled, wet scalp of the baby between her legs. "I see the top of your baby's head."

He watched the baby's head move. She pushed. His hands sweat. "Open your mouth and take short, quick breaths. Pant like a dog."

His knees were on the floor between the back and front seats. His head and shoulders were under the sheet. He wiped his sweaty hands on the sheet.

He didn't want to touch the baby because his hands weren't washed, but he had to. He had to support the baby. He rolled up his sleeves. The head came out. He cradled it with both hands.

With the next push, the baby slid into his arms. He thought, *My God, are all babies this slippery?*

He grabbed the baby's feet and turned the baby's head away from the fluid oozing from the mother. The baby wasn't breathing.

He placed the baby on the mother's abdomen, making sure the baby's head was lower than its feet. The mother's head lay back. She breathed deeply. Brand opened the baby's mouth. He massaged the infant's throat several times beginning from the bottom of its neck to its chin. Mucus came out. The baby still didn't breathe. Brand flicked the baby's little feet hard with his fingers.

The infant burst into a cry!

Brand wrapped the baby in the mother's robe and placed the infant in the mother's arms. He told her not to let loose of her baby. She nodded.

"Just relax now," he told her. "As soon as the afterbirth comes, we'll all head for the hospital. I'll signal your husband to come up to the car in a few minutes."

He knew not to pull the cord. It could tear loose from the placenta. He told the mother her birth was the best he'd ever seen. The woman smiled, her eyes never leaving her child.

"Post 93, Car 833 to Post 93."

"Go ahead, Car 833," said the lieutenant.

"Got a progress report. Few minutes ago, baby was born. We're waiting for the placenta."

"Go ahead," replied the lieutenant.

"What's the situation regardin' the plow?"

"It's a negative. Can ya get north to County 18? It's been plowed. Should be clear sailing from there to Central."

"Hope so. Gonna take least an hour before I can get to the hospital ... if I can get to 18. Request you telephone Central Receiving. Ask a doctor if I should tie off two places on the umbilical cord and cut it."

Brand thought he remembered it could take up to a half hour for the placenta to follow the baby.

"I'll check. We'll hold the info until you radio for it."

"Negative, Post 93. Radio me in the blind."

"Understood, Car 833. Will radio you in the blind just as soon as I get the information."

"Car 833 out," radioed Brand.

He returned to the back seat. The baby cried. The mother's breathing had calmed when he placed his hand on her forehead. He put the sheet under her buttocks. The cord moved three inches. A gush of blood followed. He wrapped the placenta in the sheet and placed it beside the infant.

"Post 93, Car 833 to Post 93."

"Go ahead."

"We have the placenta. Do ya have the information on the umbilical cord?"

"Standby, she's on the phone. The doctor said cut the cord. Can you copy the method?"

Brand quickly grabbed his note pad and pen. "Go ahead."

"One: with a strip of gauze from the first-aid kit, tie a square knot about four inches from where it joins the infant. Be sure to tie it tight enough so it won't leak, but not so tight your gauze cuts into the cord. Break."

"Go ahead."

"Two: use a second piece of gauze and tie it about six inches from the baby. Three: cut the cord between the two pieces of gauze. Break."

"Go ahead."

"The doctor said to keep the baby warm. If you can't get to the hospital within an hour, have the mother try to breast feed the baby. She also said to knead the uterus for about an hour. Snow is to keep up for several hours. We have nine inches now. We should get about a foot. Go ahead."

"Got it. Be en route to Central Receiving in about ten minutes. Car 833 out." He turned to the woman. "You heard the radio. There's no problem," said Brand to the mother.

He folded the gauze, tied the knots, then pulled out his penknife. He looked at the open blade. He thought, *This knife cut the seatbelt from the dead man with the swinging eyeball.* He cut the cord. He moved the placenta away from the mother and baby, then felt her abdomen. He saw the pink liquid oozing from the mother. He thought of the pink snow beside the man's hand that had fallen in front of him.

"Going to sound the siren to get your husband up here. Then we'll head for the hospital."

Brand gave the siren a short burst, and a few minutes later he saw the man struggle up the hill. When he reached the patrol car, Brand opened the door and said, "Take my place."

The man got onto the back seat.

"You warmer now?"

"Yeah, much. How's my wife?"

"Fine. Baby's fine, too. Get your hands warm. You need to massage her uterus."

The husband blew on his hands.

"Here's where to massage her," Brand said, showing him. Brand put her husband's hand over her uterus.

"You gotta massage her so she'll stop oozing. Everything looks good."

Brand eased the patrol car onto the interstate. There were no tracks to follow, but he knew the route. The baby cried.

"What's your name, folks?

"Isadora. Jim, and my wife's Gloria."

"Post 93, Car 833 to Post 93. En route to Central. Think we can make it to Route 18. Jim, Gloria, and Baby Isadora—that's Ida, Sam, Adam, David, Ocean, Robert, Adam—are in the car. We're all well."

"Good, real good," said the lieutenant.

After leaving the hospital, Brand drove to the patrol post to complete his paper work. He'd been on duty twenty hours.

"Sergeant, here's most of the paper work. Okay if I finish it at midnight when I come back on duty?"

"Yeah, still snowing like hell. You going to your apartment?" said the sergeant.

Brand nodded. "I need a shave."

"You look ragged. Forget going home. Sleep here. Nobody gives a damn what we look like in this kind of weather."

Brand kept his uniform on and crawled onto the far bunk in the room off the lockers. He slept two hours.

*   *   *

It was midnight. Brand called the pediatrics floor at Central Receiving Hospital to check on the family. "This is the Highway Patrol, Trooper Brand speaking. May I speak with someone who could give me some information on the Isadora baby?"

"Dr. Lawson speaking."

"Dr. Lawson, this is Bill Brand, Highway Patrol. I brought the Isadora family in with their baby about four hours ago. How are they doing?"

"Fine, real fine. Good job on that delivery!"

"Thanks. Doctor, I don't know whether it's a boy or a girl. I was so busy I didn't even look."

"It's a girl, six pounds four ounces!"

"How's the mother and father?"

"Mother's resting well. Don't seem to be any complications. The father's standing outside now."

"May I speak with him?"

"Sure, just a minute."

"Hello."

"Mr. Isadora?"

"Yes."

"Bill Brand here, Highway Patrol."

"Yes, yes, sir, how are you?"

"Well, thanks. I want to tell you about your car. Steel's wrecker picked it up about a half hour ago. They're located on the County Line Road at the interstate. Telephone is 829-1811."

"I wrote it down. Thank you for what you did."

"You're welcome. Glad I happened along. Congratulations to your wife and you on your new baby girl. Would you tap the button a couple of times? I'd like to speak to the switchboard."

"Switchboard."

"Would you please connect me to the psychiatric ward?"

Brand learned Proshenski was under observation and that he was calm.

Brand completed his reports at two o'clock in the morning. With the interstate closed and the storm still raging, Brand and the dispatcher were alone. All the troopers had gone home. The snow stopped about then.

Brand stepped outside in the cold, sharp air. The snow crunched and squeaked under his boots. He drove south. Two hours passed.

He was required to be on patrol until eight o'clock in the morning. It was four o'clock. His head felt the size of a grapefruit. Every few seconds, he had to shake it to stay awake. He turned his squad car north towards the patrol post. He opened his window. He needed the constant blast of frigid air to function.

When he came in, he told the dispatcher, "Log me on post to rest. I'm too tired to be on the road."

"You gotta be kidding. Just go back and sleep. The brass will be none the wiser," said the dispatcher.

"Please log me in. Wake me if it's important. If not, wake me at six."

Brand walked to the far bunk, removed his shoes, and fell asleep.

*   *   *

"Who's asleep back there?" asked the sergeant.

"Brand, sir," quickly responded the dispatcher.

Brand heard the sergeant's voice. He quelled his impulse to jump from the bed. He listened to the sergeant. "He logged on post?"

"Yes, sir ... at four o'clock. Told me to wake him at six."

"Let him sleep. He was really put through the mill yesterday. If you get anything that needs investigating, give it to me."

Brand wondered why the sergeant had come on duty so early. He closed his eyes.

The following day, each trooper worked two hours overtime because of the earlier snowstorm. *Troopers never declare overtime hours*, Brand thought, while he was completing his weekly activity sheet before going off duty. It was impressed on the cadets at the academy that claiming overtime meant one's personal time came before his devotion to duty.

Brand questioned this. He wondered how many other troopers also questioned it. He knew it was peer pressure that kept them from claiming it. He wondered if the peer pressure was real or assumed. In the column marked "Hours Overtime," he wrote "0."

*   *   *

Before he left to see Mandy, he telephoned Loretta.

"When you comin' back, Bill?" asked Loretta.

He wasn't sure what the tone in her voice meant. "Two days, Loretta."

After hanging up, he felt uneasy. He felt pressured. He didn't want to hurt Loretta, but he didn't want to be in a situation where he'd have to commit to her, answer to her.

He knocked on Mandy's door.

"If that's you, Bill, come in."

The apartment was dark. "Mandy, where are you?"

"Back here in the bedroom."

"Okay if I come back?"

"Sure, I'm getting better."

Brand walked to her bedroom. "What's the problem?"

"Flu. They gave me some pills for it earlier this week. Feeling much better now."

"Who gave you the pills?"

"A doctor at University Hospital."

"Boy, you must've been sick to go to the hospital! Why didn't ya go to health services on campus?"

"They sent me to the hospital. Now don't you worry."

"You sure?"

"Hold me."

He removed his clothes.

He gently eased next to her warm body. He knew she'd been crying.

He held her.

They slept.

"I need to get up. Just stay in bed and rest. We'll talk when you get up," said Mandy.

She locked the bathroom door.

*   *   *

"I need to tell you something I really don't want to tell you," said Mandy.

He nodded.

"I met with a Feminist Studies professor and asked her for advice. She told me men are nothing more than sperm donors, and men have no say what women do with their wombs. A woman's womb is hers alone. It's her body and her womb. A woman has the right to do whatever she wants with her body. It's not a baby until it's born. After a woman has a man's sperm, he's irrelevant. I told my doctor at University Hospital what she said, and he said I should talk with the best psychology professor on campus. I promised him I would."

Brand just listened. When she paused, he said, "Go ahead, Mandy."

"I'm so sorry to tell you this, but the psychology professor said you had a right to know what I did. I told her I'd tell you."

"What did you do?"

"The reason I went to Mexico during spring break was to have an abortion."

Brand felt emotion rising, but he didn't quite know what emotion it was. "What else did the psychology professor tell you?"

"She told me what's done is done. I couldn't undo what I'd done, but I could start being mature and not take the easy way out again by not tellin' you. She said when I got the abortion, I was a quitter, and I shouldn't compound it by being a quitter a second time by not telling you. She said quitting is addictive."

"Did she ask about the father?"

"Yes."

"What'd you say?"

"I told her he'd played basketball and was a student here. That we practically lived together until he quit school to join the highway patrol. She asked me if I was sure it was his child. I said I was. She asked me if I'd told him I was carrying our daughter what he would've done. I said he would've married me. That's true, Bill, isn't it? You would've married me?"

With mist in his eyes, he said, "Yes, Mandy, I would've married you. How'd you know it was a girl?"

"The guy in Mexico told me. There's something else the psychology professor said I needed to tell you."

Brand waited. He thought of the baby girl he'd just delivered; he thought of the little girl with the golden hair who died from the car crash.

"The reason I went to University Hospital is I got an infection in Mexico."

"You're going to get better aren't you?"

"If you mean better in the sense I'm not going to die . . . then yes. I think I'll get over the abortion, too, but I've gotta see a specialist to find out how much damage was done . . . if I can ever have a baby."

In the course of the conversation, Brand had slipped back into trooper mode. He was investigating. He was analyzing every word and the context of everything she said. He controlled the conversation by asking questions and speaking few words. "What else?"

"The professor told me the mature thing for me to do was to tell you what I'd done. I told her I would. Now that I've told you, I'm done meeting with her."

"Why?"

"She's different. She said people have to own up to their behaviors, not take the easy way out and not be a quitter because quitting is habit forming. She said I should've told you I was pregnant. We should've gotten married and provided for our daughter. If you didn't want to marry me, I should've raised her myself, or I should've given her up for adoption. She said the instant I was pregnant my responsibility shifted from me to *our* child."

"She said our child, Mandy?"

"Yes, she did, Bill."

"She said human beings are animals, and female animals protect their progeny. It's written in our genetic code."

"You said you think you'll get over the abortion. What does that mean?"

"I told the psychology professor what the professor in the Feminist Studies Department told me—that a man is nothing more than a sperm donor. The psychology professor told me a real feminist believes women and men should have equal rights and equal opportunities. She said the professor in Feminist Studies is a radical. She'd heard about her, heard that she opposes standard gender roles and advocates worldwide matriarchal societies. She said the radical feminists on campus would screw up my life more than I've already done."

Again Brand waited.

"Apparently a few radical feminists on campus are rabid man-haters. They aren't real feminists but women who want to feminize men. They despise self-confident men. She said Feminist Studies isn't an academic discipline, and professors in it have deluded themselves into thinking their department actually belongs on campus. Students shouldn't major or minor in it because it will hurt them when they apply for good-paying jobs in the real world. That her Psychology Department should offer courses in Women Studies and Men Studies."

"What you just said doesn't make sense. How you think this'll help you get over the abortion?"

"It will. Next semester, I'm taking a course in Feminist Studies. If I like it, I'm changing my major."

"You told the psychology professor this?"

"Yes."

"What'd she say?"

"She said she wasn't surprised. She called it cognitive dissonance, which is like, the more money you lose backin' a horse, the better you think the horse is. She said these so-called feminists will tell me having the abortion was the right thing to do."

"I see."

"She said people do what they do because free will is an illusion. That we're products of our genes and our environments. In her Psychology Department, faculty members are scholars who have research agendas, but she didn't try to talk me out of taking a Feminist Studies course. She just wished me well."

"You going to talk to the psychology professor again?"

"Never! I feel better about myself when I talk to women in Feminist Studies."

"What'd she say when you left her office?"

"I'm not sure, something like if I ever get my act together, to let her know, and we can talk if I want to. I don't like her."

"What's her name, Mandy?"

"Victoria Whitcombe."

*　　*　　*

While driving to see his mother, Brand thought about his visit with Mandy. How she was remorseful about the abortion and wasn't joyful like she always was the times before. She only wanted him to hold her.

He knew he could never again be close to her. If she hadn't had the abortion, he'd have been the father of a little girl. He didn't hate Mandy, didn't even dislike her. He felt she had no control over what she'd done. She seemed to be in a mist he couldn't enclose, and at the same time, it seemed like there was a vacuum where it was once filled with Mandy. He could see her, in the mist, fading away. He knew their relationship ended when she ended their daughter's life.

9

THE MATURING

THE ENVELOPE WAS FROM District Headquarters. He knew he was in trouble. There was no other reason he'd get a letter from Headquarters. He couldn't bring himself to open it. He put the envelope in his briefcase. He read the log to be updated about what took place while he was off duty. He walked slowly to his squad car and went on patrol.

He knew he'd done wrong, and he'd known when he did it he shouldn't. Still, he'd consciously done it. He had no defense.

He'd willfully violated the *Rules and Regulations* and followed up socially with a woman he'd first met in the line of duty. He'd contacted Loretta.

He wondered how they'd found out. He asked himself who would've contacted the Highway Patrol. Loretta's sister and her husband knew about him. Her parents knew. Even Mandy knew about Loretta.

He parked his squad car under a light in the rest area and took the letter from his briefcase. He knew he had to open it. He knew he'd be transferred to a post a long way from Loretta, a long way from Victoria. He opened the envelope:

Dear Trooper Brand: At 12:20 a.m. Friday, December 23 according to the facts recorded in our case 4-833-218, while checking the State Park in Sector A, you observed a motor vehicle parked on the beach, occupied by one Michael David Proshenski in an unconscious state and breathing lightly.

The expedient and systematic method in which you made your observation of the scene, the tranquilizer and gin located in the car and its presentation to the attending physician at Central Hospital, contributed greatly to an early diagnosis, treatment and complete recovery of Mr. Proshenski.

It is indeed a pleasure to commend you for exemplifying the highest tradition of the State Highway Patrol in the manner in which you carried out your investigation to a successful conclusion. Very truly yours, E. H. Robertson, Captain, Commanding Officer District 4

He put the letter back in his briefcase. He was neither relieved nor grateful for the recognition. He knew it was only a matter of time before something bad was going to happen to him. He wasn't married and wasn't in a committed relationship. But it didn't feel good having Loretta in his life. He felt as if he were tethered to a

---

stake of shame. He knew he never should've contacted her.

Brand was south of the city in his assigned area. It was eight-thirty in the morning. He patrolled the interstate at seventy miles per hour and saw in his rearview mirror a vehicle approaching at a high rate of speed. Brand stayed in the driving lane. The vehicle started to pass, then slowed, and drove into the driving lane behind his squad car. Slowly, the vehicle reduced its speed. Brand quickly drove onto the berm and slowed. The vehicle passed. Brand pulled back onto the highway and drove behind the automobile.

"Post 93, Car 833 to Post 93, file check."

"Post 93 to Car 833, go ahead."

"File check on Z 469 X."

A moment passed. "No wanted or record on Z-Zebra 469 X-ray," responded the dispatcher.

"I'll be stopping a blue Chrysler sedan bearing said registration on the interstate, just south of the city limits."

"Acknowledged. Post 93 out."

Brand drove his patrol car up to the vehicle. He observed a man driving and two women passengers. He turned on the pursuit light. The driver quickly pulled to the berm.

Before he could get out of the patrol car, the driver exited the car and started walking back to him. Because of the two women in the car, he permitted the driver to come towards him. They met midway between their two vehicles.

"Good morning, sir, may I see your driver's license and registration please?" The driver looked familiar to Brand.

"I lost my driver's license. I applied for a new one."

"Show me the application."

"John Russell Tierman, still live at . . . Tierman! Hey, I arrested you several weeks ago for speeding. Those two points should've put you at twelve. You should be under suspension. The judge took your license, didn't he?"

"Yes, but I'm not under suspension."

"How do you figure that?"

"It's my mother."

"Your mother?"

"About a week ago, she told me the middle name on my birth certificate isn't Raymond . . . it's Russell."

"I don't follow."

"The judge took my license with my incorrect name. My new license will have my correct name on it."

"Sir, the judge took your right to drive. Names don't get ticketed and get points against them. People do. You're a person, and you're driving under suspension. To get this pink-colored form you signed to get a new license, you filed a false affidavit. That's another violation."

"This can't be!"

"It is. You're under arrest. Get your hands up against the car."

"But!"

"Move it, Tierman. Now!"

He reluctantly complied. Brand searched and handcuffed him. He put him in the front seat of his patrol car. He put the seatbelt around him. He cautiously walked up to the two women sitting in the car.

"Do one of you ladies own this automobile?"

"It's my dad's." She was young and scared.

"May I see the registration, please?"

She handed it over.

"Miss Minden, do you have a valid operator's license?"

"Yes."

"May I see it?"

She gave it to him.

"Thank you." Brand saw she was sixteen years old.

"Tierman's under arrest for driving under suspension and for filing a false affidavit."

"What am I supposed to do?" she asked.

"Whatever you wish. Your friend will be at the sheriff's office in about a half hour."

"He's not our friend. We just met him."

"Is there anything in your car that belongs to him?"

The two girls looked around and shook their heads.

He wanted to tell them to stay away from Tierman, but he didn't. He left them and took Tierman in for booking. The bond was five hundred dollars.

Brand drove south on the expressway. His thoughts turned to the university, to Vicky, to Loretta, and to the studies he'd left behind toward his baccalaureate degree. He wanted to finish college. He loved the academic life and loved being around professors and college students. But he also loved the highway patrol. He wondered if the highway patrol ever granted a leave of absence to attend college.

*   *   *

"Post 93, Car 833 to Post 93."

"Go ahead, Car 833."

"I'll be checking out the rest area on the interstate, south bound. Be out of service for about fifteen minutes."

"Copy, Car 833. Post 93 out."

Brand quietly closed the door to his patrol car. He parked on the berm of the interstate to avoid being seen by anyone in the rest area. He quietly opened the door to the men's room. The door to a stall was partially open. He saw two men. One was sitting and looking down at the back of the head of a man on his knees. His buttocks faced the partially opened door of the stall.

"Gentlemen," Brand said softly.

The sitting man looked up at Brand.

"Both of you please meet me outside. I'll be waiting for you."

The man who was on his knees followed Brand. The man who was sitting didn't.

"May I have your driver's license?" Brand asked the man who had been kneeling. "Thank you. Wait for me to return."

Brand went back to the restroom.

"Mister, you get yourself out of that stall, or I'll come in and drag you out."

"Y-yes, sir. I'm coming," was the weak, frightened reply.

The three stood outside the restroom.

"Your driver's license, please," Brand said to the man who had been sitting.

"I don't have one." He started to cry.

"You've got your billfold, haven't you?"

He nodded.

"Then get it out and give me your driver's license."

"Officer, please don't do anything to me. Next month, I graduate with my Master of Divinity degree. I'm studying to be a priest. If you arrest me, it'll be my entire life. Please, officer, please."

Brand didn't speak. He looked back and forth at each man.

Brand looked at their drivers' licenses. He felt as if he were holding their lives in his hands. He took his notebook from his pocket where he wrote information for reports. But he paused there. Brand looked at the men again and at each driver's license.

He wrote nothing in his notebook. He put it back in his pocket.

He handed each man their driver's license. "Good night, gentlemen."

Brand walked to his patrol car and drove away.

"Post 93, Car 833 to Post 93."

"Go ahead."

"Back in service."

"Copy, Car 833. Any homosexuals?"

"Negative," said Brand.

He thought of Reverend Tanner. Because of what he had done to him, Brand knew he would never be at peace. He knew letting these men go wouldn't make up for what he had done to Reverend Tanner, that he never could make up for what he had done to him.

*   *   *

Brand drove to a cafe for a coffee break. He sat in the end booth with his back against the wall.

"Coffee and two doughnuts, please."

"Cream?" asked the waitress.

"Yes, please."

He knew she wouldn't accept payment because he'd tried paying her before. Brand put a dollar-fifty tip on the table, smiled, nodded at the waitress, and went back on patrol.

It was an hour after midnight. A wet, light snow fell. It stuck to the pavement. He stopped at a red light and looked south on the divided highway. He saw fresh tire tracks of a car that had weaved back-and-forth from one lane to the other. There were no other tracks. He followed them.

Within a few minutes, he saw taillights of a late model Cadillac travelling fifteen miles per hour in a fifty-mile-per-hour zone. He drove partly up on the left side of the vehicle. He didn't want to get too close for fear the motorist might weave into him. An elderly man, slouched in the seat, was driving. Brand could barely see into the vehicle. The windows were fogged. He thought the driver was either sick or intoxicated.

He tried to follow the patrol's procedure, to make sure the front of his patrol car didn't travel further ahead than the front door of the Cadillac. If he got abreast of the vehicle, the driver could weave into him. He turned on his pursuit light. The driver didn't stop. He sounded his horn. No results. He flashed his spotlight on the side of the driver's face. The driver looked straight ahead, continuing to drive at fifteen miles per hour. The driver periodically weaved off onto the berm. Brand touched his siren switch. The siren wailed. Still no reaction from the driver. He again directed his spotlight on the side of the man's face. The driver turned his head slowly and looked at the patrol car. Brand quickly turned on his dome light and motioned to the driver to pull off the roadway.

The driver stopped abruptly. His left two wheels were on the pavement, his right two wheels on the berm. Brand stopped behind him. He walked up to the motorist. The driver partially opened his window.

"May I see your driver's license and registration please?"

The driver was a heavy-set older man. Brand noticed the strong odor of a person who had been drinking alcohol exude from the half-opened window.

"Sir, your driver's license and registration, please."

The man stared ahead. He gripped his steering wheel.

"Please get out of your car."

The man looked questioningly at Brand, and then drove slowly away.

"Post 93, Car 833 to Post 93."

"Go ahead."

"I got a DWI running from me. I'm on 12, south of the city, heading south. Over."

"Want backup?"

"Negative. He just stopped again. It's a tan Cadillac bearing V 495 W."

"Copied, Car 833."

He stopped behind the Cadillac and walked up to the driver's door. Brand reached down and opened the door. Before the door could be opened fully, the motorist again drove away. Brand followed him at fifteen miles per hour. The motorist drove from the highway onto a private drive that wound among tall spruce trees, a lake, and up a hill.

"Post 93, Car 833 to Post 93."

"Go ahead."

"I need backup now. I'm on the west side of 12 one mile south of the city limits, at the end of a private lane on the top of a hill. My pursuit light is on."

"Unit 833, be advised: there are no troopers on duty. I'll call the sheriff's office and request backup."

"Copy. Car 833 out."

The "chase" ended at a stately home that overlooked the city. Brand stopped behind the Cadillac. The massive home had a four-car attached garage. The driver got out of his car and staggered toward the one open garage door.

"Highway Patrol! Stop!"

The man didn't stop. He didn't turn around. Brand couldn't allow him inside. A gun or a knife could turn a driving-under-the-influence and fleeing-a-police-officer arrest into a tragedy.

Brand took his handcuffs from his pouch. He ran to the man. "Stop! You're under arrest for fleeing a police officer!"

The man walked faster.

Brand reached down and put a handcuff on the driver's right wrist.

The man swung his free arm savagely. Brand ducked to avoid the blow.

"Hey, settle down, mister. You're just making things worse!"

"Get that handcuff off me. This is my place. You haven't the right to be here!"

Over the man's shoulder and through the trees, Brand saw the flashing red light of the sheriff deputy's squad car. It passed the driveway entrance. The man stopped struggling. He stood still, stared ahead, breathing heavily.

"Oh, my God, what's happening!?" screamed a gray-haired woman. She was in her bathrobe and ran from inside the darkened garage. Her hands were clasped to the sides of her face.

"Highway Patrol, ma'am. He's under arrest for driving under the influence and resisting arrest."

"You let my husband go! Why are you treating us this way? We're personal friends of the mayor and sheriff. Now you let him go!"

This was one of the situations Brand had been taught to avoid—being alone with a hostile man and an angry wife. He was concerned for his safety and for the health of the older man. The man's face was red. He breathed rapidly and deeply.

Brand looked to the highway. The deputies weren't coming. The drunken man jerked Brand's arm and started to walk toward the house. Brand knew he couldn't allow the man to get inside.

He quickly applied the bent-arm-bar-come-along he'd been taught at the academy. He applied pressure on the man's wrist and elbow. He tried to get him to change direction away from the house and toward the squad car. The man didn't respond like the cadets did when they practiced the hold. With his free arm, he swung again at Brand.

The gray-haired lady screamed, "Let my husband go! Let him go! Let him go!"

"Betty, get my gun!" the man screamed to his wife. "Get it and shoot him!"

Brand tripped him. He grabbed the thrashing free arm and eased the man to the ground. The man was old and stocky and strong.

The woman screamed again.

Brand put his knee on the side of his neck, pressing the man's head against the snow-covered driveway.

"Betty . . . help me," came his muffled cry.

Brand controlled the situation. He quickly hand-cuffed the free wrist. Both arms were now secured behind his back as he lay on the snow-covered drive-way. Brand looked up to locate the wife, but he didn't see her. He helped the man to his feet and walked him toward the patrol car.

"Betty, hurry," the man screamed.

Brand looked back but still didn't see the wife. He carefully placed the violator on the front seat of his squad car.

The sheriff's squad car rolled up beside Brand.

"Any problem?" one of the deputies asked.

"Maybe. The wife, she's gone inside. He told her to get a gun. He's under arrest for DWI and resisting arrest," said Brand as he nodded towards his squad car.

"Oh, my God! Don't ya know who he is?" asked the deputy.

"No. It makes no difference. He was drivin' under the influence, and he resisted arrest," said Brand.

The woman came outside. She had no gun.

"Hi, Betty, you okay?" asked the deputy.

She screamed, "He's got Charlie! Nick, tell him to let Charlie go!"

Brand buckled the seatbelt around the violator. The man was secure with his hands cuffed behind him and the seatbelt tightly fastened.

"Tell her I'm taking him in for booking. She can get him out in six hours when he's sober."

Brand got in his squad car, turned off the pursuit light and drove down the lane. The passenger's face was flushed. His breathing was relaxed. He was asleep.

"Post 93, Car 833 to Post 93."

"Go ahead, Car 833."

"Be advised I've got a male in the car. First name Charles, last name unknown, en route for booking on DWI and resisting arrest, over."

"Copied, Car 833. Post 93 out."

Brand helped him from the patrol car. He saw the seat of his squad car was damp where the man had been sitting.

Brand removed the handcuffs when they reached the booking desk. The booking officer paused. He looked at Brand's nameplate above his badge. He looked into Brand's eyes.

"Listen here, officer, you be polite to me. I'm Mr. Charles Goodhue," he said to the booking officer.

"Mr. Goodhue," said Brand, "I have an Alcoholic Influence Report I'd like to complete, and I want to give you the opportunity to take a Breathalyzer test. Before I ask you any questions, you must understand your rights: You have the right to remain silent. You are not required to say anything to me, nor are you required to answer any questions. Anything you do or say may be used against you in a court of law. You have the right to talk to a lawyer before I ask you any questions, and you may have him with you during questioning. If you cannot afford an attorney, the court will provide you an attorney free of charge. If you want to go ahead and answer questions without a lawyer present, you still have the right to stop answering at any time you wish. Do you understand your rights, Mr. Goodhue, as I've explained them to you?"

"Yes, officer."

"That's it, Charlie. Don't say another word. Betty called me." The man speaking to the defendant had been standing by the drinking fountain watching everything Brand did and had listened to Brand give Goodhue his Miranda warning. "Officer, my name is Byrd. Mrs. Goodhue called me when you and Mr. Goodhue were in their driveway. I'll be serving as his attorney."

"Is that correct, Mr. Goodhue?" asked Brand.

He nodded.

"Okay, I have a Breathalyzer in my briefcase. Would you give me a sample of your breath for analysis?"

Goodhue looked at his attorney. His attorney shook his head. Goodhue mimicked his lawyer.

"Would you like to submit to an oral interview?"

Goodhue looked at his attorney, then shook his head.

"Would you like to do some physical performance tests?"

Goodhue shook his head.

"I understand. Please come with me. I'm finished. He's ready for processing," said Brand to the booking officer.

Again, the booking sergeant looked into Brand's eyes.

Brand booked him on charges of driving under the influence and resisting arrest.

The booking officer nodded goodbye to Brand as Brand walked to the elevator. He heard the booking officer say the bond was one thousand dollars.

* * *

Brand thought of what Victoria said to him at their first meeting.

"Quitting is addictive. Quitting is habit forming. Quitting is a bad personality trait. Don't you be a quitter, Bill."

He knew he was a quitter.

Brand thought, *"Quitter" is an ugly word, an ugly and offensive word. Dad made me quit football when I was a sophomore in high school. He said to focus on basketball because I'd never be good enough to get a college scholarship for football. I had no choice. I had to quit football and play basketball.*

Brand remembered his father's words: "When you put your feet under my table and eat my food, you will do what I say. If you don't like it, there's the door." He had no choice then. He had a choice now.

He thought, *I love the highway patrol. I love college, but I quit college. Yes, Victoria, you were right. I'm a quitter. I should've stayed in college and joined the highway patrol after I'd graduated.*

Brand submitted a letter of request for a leave of absence to finish college.

* * *

"My office," said the lieutenant. "Close the door." When they were seated, the lieutenant said, "Bill, I saw the disposition of the Goodhue case. It was dismissed because you didn't appear in court. You didn't show up for the hearing. What the hell happened?"

"Dismissed! Sir, that can't be! We weren't notified of the new time and day of the hearing.

"His attorney got three continuances. Each time the clerk phoned and gave us the new time and date of the hearing. They're typed on the log. But we were never notified the time and date when the last hearing was set. The clerk of court never called. He didn't notify us," said Brand.

"Stand by . . . I'll check the log."

The lieutenant returned and closed his office door. "You're right. We weren't notified."

"What we do now, sir?"

"Nothing!"

"Nothing, sir! Goodhue drove drunk, fled a police officer, and resisted arrest . . . and we do nothing?"

"Yeah, we do nothing."

"That's not fair, lieutenant! His attorney could sue me and the Highway Patrol."

"He won't."

Brand looked at the lieutenant.

"Bill, I know it's not fair. Years ago I was in a similar situation when I was young like you. My lieutenant told me I'd learn that life wasn't fair."

"Why won't he take this to civil court?"

"I read your Goodhue file. You did everything right. You had him cold. His attorney will advise him he already pulled strings to beat the charges. If he sues us, we'll hang Byrd and Goodhue out to dry. Goodhue and Byrd are too important to risk the publicity."

*   *   *

Brand didn't question the lieutenant's logic assigning him to the hard-up area of the district. He figured the lieutenant thought the chances of his finding another high-profile person in that section of the city and surrounding countryside unlikely.

Brand worked the 6:00 p.m. to 2:00 a.m. shift. It was dusk. He drove west on an inner-city street when an east-bound vehicle with four men drove by him. The passenger in the left rear seat grinned and gave Brand the finger.

Brand rose to the bait. He said to himself, *You can't give the finger to a state trooper!*

Brand stopped, backed into an alley, and turned around. It was almost dark. He followed the vehicle. Suddenly, the driver made a left turn down a street known for drugs, prostitutes, and rough bars. The driver made the left turn without signaling.

Brand turned on his pursuit light. The car slowed, but didn't stop. He tapped his horn. The car didn't stop. Brand touched the siren switch. The siren yowled. The car stopped in the middle of the street. Without thinking, Brand turned on his outside speaker and walked up to the car.

"Good evening, sir. You were stopped for failing to signal your left turn. May I see your driver's license and registration, please?"

Brand knew this was no place to be. Giving a trooper the finger wasn't a violation of law, but failing to signal a turn was. He focused only on the four men. He didn't take his eyes from them.

"Ain't you got your quota yet?" the driver said loudly.

Brand briefly took his eyes from the driver and passengers. He saw both sides of the street filling with onlookers. He was surrounded.

He had committed one of the police officer's deadly sins. He had lost situational awareness.

"Why you here, statie-man? You got to be a crazy man to come here alone. When the cops come down here, man, they come in force."

He suppressed his impulse to say he wasn't alone. *There are seven of us here, one trooper and six rounds of .38 caliber bullets in his revolver.* He looked at the driver's license. He did this only for the spectators that had surrounded him and his squad car. He wanted to show that he wasn't harassing them, that he was just doing his job.

"Everything here is fine, sir. Please be sure to signal your turns in the future. Thank you for your consideration."

Brand handed the license and registration back to the driver. The driver, his passengers, and onlookers glared at Brand. Brand didn't return their glares. He turned and walked to his patrol car. He instantly turned off the outside speaker that was broadcasting loudly, and the pursuit light flashing and bathing red into all the windows. Those, he thought, along with the single wail of the siren had brought all the people out on the sidewalks and street. Brand slowly drove away. He knew he had been stupid. He'd elevated the status of the man who gave him the finger. He remembered what he'd thought about saying to Professor Smalley. *No one my equal would offend me, and no one beneath me could offend me.* He knew he should've just smiled and nodded to the man who gave him the finger. He'd been lucky.

*   *   *

It was spring. He could now drive with his window open. He'd tried all sorts of home remedies to remove Goodhue's urine smell from his patrol car. Still, he considered himself lucky he'd yet to experience a drunk vomiting all over him and all over the inside of his patrol car.

There was no quota, but every trooper knew he should give around thirty traffic tickets a month. Before his new patrol area assignment, Brand had ticketed around fifty people a month. Now, he wrote around twenty tickets. He hoped the lieutenant would understand this decrease. Earlier, Brand would ticket or arrest anyone if the violation warranted it. Now, it was different.

*   *   *

At one-thirty in the morning, Brand saw a man waving his arms and motioning for him to stop. Brand knew this could be a trap, an ambush.

Brand stopped about twenty yards from the man. He ran towards Brand. Brand quickly put his right hand under his jacket, and into the inside vest pocket where he had a concealed semi-automatic pistol. He partially opened his window. His thumb rested on the safety. The pistol was aimed at the man's chest. He could fire immediately. If there were no threat, the man would never know Brand had a pistol under his jacket aimed at his chest.

"Officer, would ya give me a ride to my car?"

The man was frightened and out of breath.

"What's the problem?"

Brand cautiously watched him, his thumb on the safety.

"Got rolled. All I want is a ride to my car. It's about six blocks back up that way parked in an alley."

"What were you doing up there?"

"In town on business. Met this woman . . . she rolled me." He now looked more embarrassed than frightened.

"Okay, get in."

Brand started toward the man's car. "You should file charges," he told the man. "I can take you to the city police station, if you want?"

"Forget that! All I want is my car."

"Well, at least tell me how it happened. I'm a state trooper. We're inside the city limits, so I won't have to file any paper."

"Promise?"

"Yeah, I'm just interested. Tell me how it happened."

"Well . . . I picked her up down the street from where I saw you. She told me where to drive. We did a little playin' around, and then she grabbed my billfold. She ran down between those buildings."

"How'd she get your billfold?"

"I don't have to tell you."

"That's right, you don't, and I don't have to take you to your car."

"The bitch wanted to haggle about money, so I took out my billfold. She grabbed it and took off."

"Why didn't you run after her?"

"By the time I got my pants up, I couldn't see where she'd gone. She started runnin' down that way," said the man, pointing. "I ran down there chasin' her. That's when I saw you."

"Did ya consider her a bitch when ya picked her out to have sex with you?"

He didn't answer.

"Well, there's your car. I'll follow you for your safety until you get out of this neighborhood."

He nodded, got out of the squad car, and drove away. Brand followed him until he reached the highway.

Yes, Victoria, we're animals, thought Brand.

10

THE SEASONING

WEEKS PASSED. There was no reply from General Headquarters about the leave.

"Here's a warrant to serve. His name's John Jones," said the sergeant, who handed Brand the warrant. Jones had failed to appear in court for reckless operation and driving under suspension. Brand would serve the warrant, arrest him, book him, and take his driver's license.

He remembered once before trying to serve an arrest warrant at a house in the hard-up area of the district. When he knocked, people ran out the back door and jumped from windows.

At 7:55 a.m., Brand phoned John Jones.

"Good morning, this is the Revelation Law Firm. May I speak with Mr. John Jones, please?" said Brand.

"He ain't here," replied a female voice.

"With whom am I speaking?"

"This here's his woman."

"Oh, very fine, Mrs. Jones, I have a check for Mr. Jones in the amount of two-thousand-two-hundred-seventy-two dollars and seventy-seven-cents. It's his share of the estate of Mr. William G. Reckless. Do you know where I can find Mr. Jones? We need his signature, and then I can give him the check."

"He jest came in the door. Jest a minute, mister."

"Hello. Hello. John Jones at this end."

"Mr. John Jones of 418 Howard Street?"

"Yes, sir. Him aspeakin'."

"Excellent, Mr. Jones. Did you know Mr. William G. Reckless? You did some work for him several years ago."

"Yes, sir, I sure do."

"Excellent, Mr. Jones. I'm sorry to inform you that Mr. Reckless died six months ago. In his will he left you the money he owed you. The check is for $2,272.77. His will stated this is the amount he owed you for work you did for him several years ago. If we found you Mr. Reckless wanted us to tell you that he tried to find you, but he wasn't successful in locating you, Mr. Jones.

"Is the amount stated the correct amount, Mr. Jones?"

"Yes, sir, sure is!"

"Excellent, Mr. Jones. I need you to sign an affidavit in front of a notary. Our law firm has spent a good deal of time finding you, Mr. Jones, and we'd like to give you the check as soon as possible. Can you come down to the courthouse and sign for the check this morning?"

"Sure can."

"How about ten o'clock this morning? Just give your name to the woman at the reception desk when you come through the front doors. Ask her for directions to the Revelation Law Firm."

"Okay, I be there!" said Jones.

"Oh, Mr. Jones, I almost forgot. The notary will need to see some identification. Please bring your passport."

"Ain't got no passport!" said Jones.

"Well, she'll need to see some type of government-issued identification that has your picture on it."

"Got a driver's license," said Jones.

"That'll work just fine, Mr. Jones. Bring that."

Brand hung up the phone and walked to his patrol car. While driving to the courthouse, Brand thought about how he and Trooper Lakes questioned this method of picking up people on misdemeanor arrest warrants. Brand had tried to serve warrants in a more conventional manner months before. He'd go at night, locate the house or apartment, and knock on the door. If the door opened, he'd usually be speaking with the person in a dimly lit hallway. Through the opened door, he'd hear people in the house or apartment whispering and moving around. But that wasn't enough "probable cause" to enter. The person he was speaking to would simply deny any knowledge of the individual named in the warrant. Brand knew after he left, the person would tell the wanted individual a trooper was looking for him, and the trooper had an arrest warrant. When the individual knew there was a warrant for him, he'd be harder to catch. And catch was a good name for it, Brand knew. He saw his job when serving an arrest warrant as a hunter pursuing prey.

Brand parked the patrol car two blocks from the courthouse, so he wouldn't give Jones any reason to be suspicious. He walked to the courthouse. It was 9:15 a.m.

He greeted the receptionist.

"Hi, Irene."

"Mornin', Bill."

"There'll be a John Jones, around forty, coming in a little before ten."

"Same procedure?" she asked, smiling.

"Yup. Thanks."

She knew the routine. She did it well. This was her day job. Her night job was a high-end call girl. She wanted to stay in good with the police.

Brand got off the elevator at the tenth floor. He picked up the telephone receiver by the elevator door and held it as if he were talking to keep others from using the phone. He depressed the button, so the phone could ring. At 9:45 it rang.

"He's comin' up. White shirt and gray slacks."

"Thanks, Irene."

There was no one in the hallway. Brand was relieved he didn't have to clear it. The elevator door opened. John Jones walked out. Brand waited for the elevator door to close. Jones stood in the hallway. Brand walked up to him.

"Mr. Jones, Highway Patrol. I have a warrant for your arrest . . . up against the wall."

The perplexed man obeyed. Brand searched and handcuffed him. He escorted him out the rear of the building to avoid passing Irene. He took him to the county jail, booked him, and took his driver's license.

* * *

"You're all alike, you damned bastards!"

Brand stopped at the traffic light. A man was berating a city police officer. Brand pulled to the curb. He walked up to the officer. "Can I help?"

"Yeah, go back to my squad car and call a wrecker. He just donated his car to us."

"What you talkin' about?" asked Brand.

"Listen, trooper, don't let him do it," said the driver. "That prick wants my car!"

"Ah, forget it. I'll call the wrecker myself. Watch him."

The city police officer walked back to his cruiser.

"You know what he did?" asked the driver.

Brand shook his head. "No, and it's none of my business either."

"That bastard walked up to me while I was parked here. He tossed a bag of coke in my car. That's what the sonofabitch did!"

"You expect me to believe that! If he operated that way, he'd never get a conviction. Who you trying to kid?"

"Well, you're a dumb bastard? How long you been a statie?" said the man.

Brand felt uneasy. *Surely this city police officer is better at finding evidence than having to resort to planting it.* The officer walked back to where the man and Brand were standing.

"He giving you any trouble?"

"No. But he's got one helluva story, though."

"Probably told you I dropped a bag in his car, didn't he?" said the officer.

"Yeah," said Brand.

The city police officer looked at the man, and said, "You're all alike. Lie like hell."

The driver said nothing. He glared at the police officer. He glared at Brand.

The wrecker arrived.

"Well, this'll make our department a real nice car. You got a bar in the back of this Caddie?" asked the police officer.

Brand looked briefly at the officer's face for a clue why he spoke so cruelly to the man.

"Whatya talking about? This car stolen?" asked Brand.

"Hell no. Anytime enough dope is found in a car, the dope and the car are confiscated."

*   *   *

Brand met Lakes at the patrol post when they were going off duty.

"Hey, Ron, got a question for ya."

"Sure, Bill, what's up?"

"Came across an interesting situation this morning. A city police officer arrested a fellow for possession of coke. He said he had it in his car."

"Was it a Lincoln or Cadillac?"

"Cadillac . . . how'd ya guess, Ron?"

"Guess we never covered this. The city cops had good evidence the guy is dirty. They've been trying to arrest him for a long time for selling drugs, but couldn't legally catch him. So, they set him up."

"How?"

"You said this happened about an hour ago, right?"

Brand nodded.

"That surprises me. This kinda thing usually goes down at night. What happens is the guy is a confirmed dope dealer. He's so good at not getting caught with the dope on him they target him. They start trailing him. When the time's right, a snitch or an officer has a bag of coke tucked in his hand. He walks up to the car where the man's sitting, makes small talk, puts his hands on the window sill, and discreetly drops the bag in the car . . . and the dope dealer's history."

"Come on, Ron, we both know this wouldn't get to first base in court . . . unless the police officer lies under oath."

Lakes said nothing.

"The city officer said the city takes his car," said Brand.

"Yeah, there's a federal statute that permits vehicles to be confiscated in these types of situations."

"What they do with them?"

"The cars? You'd be surprised at some of the automobiles city and county officials drive. They're real nice Caddies and Lincolns. Detectives use some for unmarked cars, too. Those they don't want, they auction off."

"Hey, heard your leave will be coming through tomorrow."

Brand said, "No kidding! How'd you hear it?"

"Down at District Headquarters yesterday when it arrived from GHQ."

"Sure gonna miss this, Ron."

"You'll be back." Lakes gave Brand an odd look, then said, "I wanna say something to ya, Bill."

"Go ahead, Ron."

"You're a good trooper, a different kind of trooper, but a good trooper. I liked being your field-training officer, but there's something."

"Go ahead, Ron." Brand hoped he wasn't going to say he'd heard about Loretta.

"What I need to say is you're too aggressive. You've the knack of getting yourself into situations that, someday, will get you injured or killed. I worry about you, Bill. It's good you're going on leave. The lieutenant, sergeants, and I have talked about this. We don't know why so many situations happen to you that don't happen to other troopers, but they do."

"Maybe the reason is I've kinda got a missionary zeal about things I love. I love being a state trooper. To me, it's kinda like being a teacher and a social worker at the same time. The difference is a trooper can help people more directly and more immediately. I had a professor say some people have obsessive-compulsive disorders and some people have obsessive-compulsive traits. I know I've an obsessive-compulsive trait. My brain just won't let me slack off."

"Did you love basketball the way you love college and the patrol?"

"Oddly, Ron, didn't care for it. Didn't like being in the limelight. I played for dad. Never liked the attention basketball brought me. Don't know why it brings joy to people to play a game where your goal is to win. Winning makes a lot of people feel bad because they lost. Had a professor say it's because we still have primitive brains. It's instinctual to want to dominate other people. She said sports were less lethal than tribal warfare, but serves the same purpose, and our brains don't know the difference, that we're still naked apes."

"Well, I said what I wanted to say. Now, it's on to something else for you. What were ya studying when you quit college to go to the academy?"

"Finished my general education requirements. Thinking about majoring in philosophy."

"Well that's strange. I figured you'd say criminal justice. Why philosophy?"

"You know, Ron, the more I'm out here around people who just consistently screw up, the more I believe they can't help it. I believe nature didn't give them much to work with. In fact—and don't go thinkin' I'm nuts now—but I wonder if any of us really make choices in life. Maybe we're just dealt a hand at conception and add the experiences we have in life, and that's who we are. Maybe, just maybe, Ron, this feeling we make choices is only an illusion, and our brains evolved this way to trick us. Maybe there's no such thing as free will. We could be just actors in a play blind to the fact we're acting out a script written by our genes and our environments."

Lakes clapped him on the back. "When you find out, let me know. Right now, I can do my job as a trooper because I believe people make choices. If what you say is true, then our justice system will need to change," said Lakes.

"Remember the time I arrested those two homosexuals, the minister and the truck driver? My God, Ron, that bothers me still. I have trouble sleeping for thinking of what I did. They couldn't help themselves. They were born that way. What if what I did made him lose his church? I'll never be able to make up for what I did to him."

"Bill, you're thinking way too much. Let's say you're right and they were born homosexual. They still should've controlled themselves, and they sure as hell should have stayed out of the rest area."

"Even if that's true, Ron, when a man and woman are making out in the rest area and are indecently exposed or engaging in sodomy, we don't arrest them. If they're born heterosexual and they have their pants down, even if they're with people not their spouses, we walk away and let them make out. If they're born homosexual and have their pants down, we don't walk away. We arrest them for indecent exposure, or, if we see penetration, for sodomy."

"Maybe you'll find we're doing it all wrong."

"Most everything else we do seems right."

"This bothers you way too much," said Lakes. "Why don't you find out if he lost his church?"

"How would I go about it?"

Lakes rubbed his chin. "Well, you'd have to be careful. You could get him in big trouble if he's still the minister there and your inquiry points him out as a homosexual all over again. You know the name of the church?"

Brand nodded. "Yup, I know it."

"I remember he was from Winchester. It's a small town, so call another church in Winchester. Ask if anyone knows of a church in town that recently hired a new minister," said Lakes.

"Then what?"

"If you're told it's the same church where he was the minister, ask who the new minister is and ask for the church's phone number."

"Then what?"

"This is where it gets touchy. Telephone the church and ask to speak with the new minister."

"Okay, then what?"

"Ask to speak with him confidentially. If he agrees, explain you're the trooper who arrested the previous minister, that you did what you were told to do, but you felt bad when you did it, and it still bothers you."

*   *   *

Brand telephoned the Methodist Church in Winchester. The minister told Brand to telephone the church where he knew the minister he had arrested had been the minister.

When he made the second call, a woman's voice said, "Hello, Reverend Williams speaking."

"Reverend Williams, the receptionist at the Methodist Church gave me your name and number."

"Thank you for calling. How may I help you?"

"I'm wondering how Reverend Tanner is doing?"

The woman paused, then said, "Why you wondering?"

"Could I drive over and talk with you about it?"

"Perhaps, but first tell me why you're wondering how he is?"

"I did something I wish I hadn't done?"

"What'd you do?"

"May our conversation be kept confidential?"

"Yes. Now tell me what you did!"

"I'm the trooper who arrested Reverend Tanner for indecent exposure. I did what we had been told to do, but right after I arrested him, it didn't feel right, and I can't get it out of my mind what I did. He told me if I arrested him he'd lose his church. Apparently that's true."

"What's your name?"

"Trooper Bill Brand. I'm posted about a hundred miles from Winchester."

"Thank you for confiding in me, Trooper Brand. Please call me back tomorrow morning at nine o'clock."

"I will."

Brand spent another restless night with Reverend Tanner on his mind, now with the added feelings that he had, indeed, cost the man his church. At nine o'clock in the morning, he telephoned Reverend Williams.

"Good morning, Reverend Williams. This is Bill Brand."

"Good morning, Bill. I was hoping you'd call back. I was thinking all day yesterday what I was going to say to you."

That made Brand uncomfortable. "Yes, go ahead."

"I'll speak with you, but only face to face."

"I have two days off starting tomorrow. Could drive over tomorrow or Wednesday."

"Too soon. How about two weeks from tomorrow at eleven o'clock in the morning at the church."

"That'll work for me. I'll be there two weeks from tomorrow at eleven o'clock. Thank you, Reverend Williams."

"You're welcome, Bill."

*   *   *

He slept only a few hours each day. He worked the midnight-to-eight shifts, but he couldn't sleep during the day because he couldn't stop thinking about what he'd done and about why the minister wanted him to wait so long before seeing her.

He had to fight to stay awake during his midnight-to-eight shifts. He'd never been this tired and this fretful.

He slowed for a stop sign in a rural area when he saw a vehicle speeding through the intersection. It was half-past two in the morning.

Brand turned and followed, catching up to the vehicle quickly. He paced it at over seventy miles per hour.

When the driver saw him, he slowed to forty-five miles per hour. Brand motioned the driver to pull over under a street light on a freshly graveled parking area. Six people crowded the rusty vehicle. It had an out-of-state license plate. Brand approached slowly and with utmost caution.

"Good morning, sir. May I see your driver's license and registration, please?"

The driver stared straight ahead and didn't move. A heavyset older woman in a house dress sat next to him, and an older man sat on the other side of the woman. Three children sat in the back seat. No one in the car spoke. No one in the car moved. They all stared straight ahead.

A little more forcefully, Brand said, "Sir, your driver's license and registration, please."

The driver's head fell slightly. Then he turned and looked at Brand. "Officer, haven't got one. I'm under suspension."

"Please come back to the patrol car, so we can talk."

Brand quickly walked to his squad car. He watched the driver approach him.

"Sir, put your hands against the car and spread your legs. You're under arrest for driving under suspension."

The driver put his hands against the patrol car. Because the driver's shoes slipped on the pea gravel, Brand couldn't unbalance him by moving his feet backwards and spreading his legs to the correct position to properly search him. But just as Brand reached for him with one hand and his handcuffs with the other, the driver ran. His feet dug into the pea gravel, spraying it back on Brand.

Brand reflexively pulled his revolver. "Stop or I'll shoot!"

The driver didn't stop.

Brand had a perfect sight picture between the shoulders of the man's back. He began to squeeze the trigger.

"*Please don't kill my baby!*" screamed the mother.

Brand instantly raised his gun skyward. He took his finger off the trigger. The driver ran around a building.

Brand was stunned. He stared after the escaped driver and shook his head.

He remembered pulling his revolver. He remembered yelling, "Stop or I'll shoot." He remembered the perfect sight picture. He remembered squeezing the trigger. He knew he had done those things, but he didn't know why.

Then the mother had yelled. It was if her voice had suddenly returned him to normal, and he couldn't fathom why he pulled his revolver and was actually prepared to shoot a man for driving under suspension. He felt as if he'd awaken from a horrendous dream.

He holstered his weapon and walked back to the car.

"Either of you have a driver's license?"

"I do," said the man sitting next to the mother.

Brand didn't ask to see it. "You may leave. I'll look for your son. Please know I won't hurt him if I find him, but I'll arrest him for driving under suspension. Does he know a phone number where he can reach you?"

"Tell him we'll be home in six hours," said the mother.

"If I find him, I'll tell him. You may go now."

A half hour passed when Brand saw the driver walking. Brand hid his squad car behind a building, got out and waited for the driver to walk by him.

He arrested and booked him for driving under suspension.

*   *   *

When the day came to go to Winchester, Brand wore street clothes and drove his truck. When his knock on the door was answered, he said, "I'm Bill Brand."

Reverend Williams said, "Thank you for coming, Bill. Let's go upstairs to my office."

When they were seated, she said, "The reason I pushed out our meeting for two weeks was I wanted to talk to his mother before I talked to you. She gave me these."

Reverend Williams opened her desk drawer and pulled out two crucifixes. "This large one his mother wanted me to have. This small one she wanted me to give to you."

Reverend Williams slid the small crucifix across her desk. Brand picked it up. He said, *It's the crucifix he had cupped in his hands when he prayed and begged me not to arrest him!*

Brand took a deep breath. "They replaced him, didn't they? He did lose his church, didn't he, Reverend Williams?"

"Yes."

"How?"

"It's not important you know."

"Please tell me what happened."

Reverend Williams seemed to struggle. She began slowly. "He was different. He had the Stations of the Cross on the walls of the church. He had a difficult time relating to the parishioners. He talked way above their heads. He thought too much, and he did odd things. His mother said, 'My son would've been more at peace if he'd been a priest.'"

Brand didn't really understand. "Can you give me another example how he was different?" he asked.

"At two o'clock in the morning, he'd turn on his car lights to cut the grass with a power mower. It woke the neighbors," she said.

"Will he get another church more in line with his intellect and personality?" asked Brand.

She paused, now clearly uncomfortable. She looked at Brand and said in the barest whisper, "No."

"What'll he do?"

"Don't ask, Bill. Please don't. It doesn't matter."

Brand burst out, "I ruined his life, and it doesn't matter? It *does* matter!"

The woman minister's face firmed. "No, Bill, it really doesn't. Did anyone ever tell you that *you* think too much, that you ask too many questions? Not all questions have answers, and some that do don't have nice ones."

"I know I ask a lot of questions, but—"

"Don't you know the greater your wisdom the greater your grief? Increasing knowledge only increases sorrow?"

"I'd think it'd be the other way around. He who increases knowledge increases contentment," said Brand.

"Not so, Bill . . . from the Bible . . . Ecclesiastes 1:18."

Brand nodded. He didn't need to argue philosophy.

"Just let it go. You did what you were supposed to do. You followed orders."

"Yes, but sometimes following an order is the wrong thing to do."

"Give me an example," said Reverend Williams.

"We see straight people in rest areas indecently exposed, and we don't arrest them, so why do we arrest homosexuals? People born homosexual can't help their orientation any more than straight people can help theirs."

After a moment of thought, Reverend Williams said, "Okay, Bill, I'll tell you what happened, if you really want me to."

"I do."

"You arrested Reverend Tanner. The next day, when the cleaning lady went into the church, she found him dead."

Brand's mouth dried out. "How'd he die?"

"He killed himself on the church altar. The crucifix his mother gave me was over his heart. The crucifix she wanted me to give you was in his hand."

Brand thrust himself to his feet. "I'll never atone," he said.

The minister also rose and reached for his hand. "You will," she said sincerely. "You will."

Tears had found Brand's eyes. "How will I? I killed a man. I killed a man with my words and actions!"

"Don't be so hard on yourself," she said.

"Hard? No. I'll never atone. How will I?"

"Serve people. Find people who need help and help them. Do it quietly. Seek no attention from anyone for the good you do. If you want to be recognized for your good deeds, you negate the good you've done. Desiring recognition isn't Christian. It's prideful. Pride is a deadly sin."

Brand looked at her.

"Do good without recognition. Wanting recognition is self-centered. Being self-centered will destroy your soul," said Reverend Williams. Her tone was soothing but firm.

"What I did caused a man to die for something he had no control over."

"Reverend Tanner had no control over what he wanted, but you're forgetting you had no control over what you did. You'd had orders. No one has free will, Bill. Only God does. It was God's will you arrest Reverend Tanner."

Brand screwed up his face. "You saying it was God's will he commit suicide?"

Reverend Williams said, "The reason I wanted to see you face to face, Bill, is that I needed to know you as a man. I believe you have the intellect to understand what I'm going to say next." She paused and looked into his eyes. "God knows precisely what's going to happen to each and every one of us."

"You saying God had a hand in Reverend Tanner's suicide?"

Her expression was serious but steady. "Yes. God could've stopped him. He didn't."

Brand looked down at Reverend Tanner's silver-and-black crucifix that *now was cradled in his hands*. He looked at Reverend Williams. "Just like God could've stopped Jesus from being crucified, but he didn't."

She nodded.

"The Bible says this about us mortal humans in Psalm 139, Verse 4: 'You know what I am going to say even before I say it, Lord.' God knows what we're going to say and going to do even before we know what we're going to say and going to do."

"Then there's no free will," said Brand.

"God gives us this illusion of free will so we can feel ownership for what we do, so that we have peace of mind, and we can feel we are in control of our lives. There's a Woody Allen witticism we ministers like to say to each other. Wanna hear it?"

He nodded.

"Wanna know how to make God laugh? Tell him your plans."

Brand smiled. "It would help if you give me your definition of God."

"Order in the universe. Order in the universe is God's divine plan. Don't do anything with the hope of being appreciated. Don't seek attention. Don't desire recognition for the good you do. Don't talk about the good you do. Ibsen wrote, 'A thousand words leave not the same deep impression as does a single deed.' Live your life that way, Bill."

"Life's multidimensional and ephemeral, isn't it, Reverend Williams?"

She smiled and nodded. "Bill, I feel like I've known you a long time. Please call me Marlene."

He nodded.

"When you get the chance, see the movie *Magnificent Obsession*. It'll show you what I'm talkin' about," said Marlene.

"How?"

"It's complex."

He looked at her inquiringly.

"It's inspirational. I don't want to give away the plot. You'll see. Trust me. It's a film by Douglas Sirk . . . stars Rock Hudson, Agnes Moorhead, and Jane Wyman. They're showin' it at the Paramount at one," said Marlene. She looked at her watch, then looked at Brand. "Starts in an hour. Wanna go?"

"I'll drive," said Brand.

11

THE MAN

BRAND WONDERED if what Marlene said about Reverend Tanner's suicide made him feel this way or if what happened between Victoria and him caused it or if Mandy's abortion had been the deciding factor. Regardless, he knew he would no longer be upset about events that happened to him. He knew what mattered was what he told himself about those events.

He wondered about having a ready-made family, wondered if a woman with a child made a difference or if the man marrying a widow would be compared to her dead husband. Was it Loretta's intense beauty that captivated him? If Loretta and he married would her first husband's ghost follow him throughout his life?

Sixty-one days passed since he'd seen Mandy, since he'd learned she'd terminated their little girl. He wouldn't cross off the sixty-second day on his calendar until he left for duty at eleven o'clock. He missed her.

He'd had a dormitory room when he was in college, but most nights were spent with her in her apartment.

He wondered if he ever saw her on campus what he'd feel and what he'd say. He knew logic had nothing to do with what *she* had done, that logic had nothing to do with what *he* had done. Mandy's abortion ended their daughter's life. His arrest ended the minister's life.

He wondered if he, she, and all people were nothing but creatures of emotion, if everyone were self-absorbed, easily offended children who lived their lives with the illusion that they were in charge of themselves. Deep down human brains evolved to give the illusion that people made choices so they could have peace of mind—nature's and God's way to keep people breeding and evolving.

He thought of Victoria saying in class her definition of God is order in the universe. She believed in God in that nature, God, and order in the universe were synonymous. If it weren't for cognitive dissonance, people couldn't live with themselves for the shame they'd feel from the decisions they made and the people they hurt. He thought about Reverend Williams quoting the Bible verse that increasing knowledge increases sorrow, that maybe it was better to not think too much.

Now, he'd be returning to the university, to where Mandy was and Victoria was. Had they used him, or had he used them? Maybe everyone just used everyone, and that was the nature of humans, of all animals.

Brand looked at his watch. He'd worked four hours of overtime. He wished he could get overtime pay or at least get the hours worked back in time off. The unwritten rule wouldn't permit that.

* * *

"Officer, there's a woman standing over two bodies about two blocks down the street. She's holding a gun!"

"Which side of the street?"

"Other side," the man responded excitedly, pointing.

Before Brand drove the patrol car from the gas station, he made a mental note of the man's license-plate number. He'd been on duty two hours and had just finished refueling. It was two o'clock in the morning. He turned off his headlights, wanting surprise to be in his favor. In situations like these, he knew red lights and sirens were only for television. In the real world, they caused too much notice.

"Post 93, Car 833 to Post 93."

"Go ahead!"

"Motorist bearing license number Victor 487 Tom just advised this unit of a woman with a gun standing over two bodies on Market Avenue two blocks west of Howard Street. Coming up on it now. Notify city police immediately. Over."

"Acknowledged. Will notify and run a registration check."

Brand stopped his patrol car twenty yards from the scene to survey the situation. A woman, dressed in a suit and holding a gun, looked down at two men on the sidewalk. Brand quietly exited his squad car, crouched behind the car's door, and directed his spotlight on the woman. His revolver's sights were trained directly on the woman's chest.

"Highway Patrol. Freeze!"

"Hey, it's okay, trooper. I'm Detective Parks, City Police!"

"Lay down that gun slowly!" ordered Brand.

She moved carefully. She gently placed the revolver on the sidewalk. "Take it easy, trooper. Look down the street at the corner. That's our black-and-white-squad. We've already got our perp under arrest."

Brand kept his revolver trained on the woman who said she was a detective. He turned his head slightly to see if there was a police car. Two officers sat in the front. A man sat in the back. Their dome light was on.

"Don't you move a muscle until I check this out," ordered Brand.

"Just stay cool, trooper. Just stay cool," she said, standing on the sidewalk.

Brand reached his right foot into his car and tapped the siren switch. The city police officer behind the wheel of the squad car rolled down his window.

"Hey, she all right?" yelled Brand.

"Yeah, she's our detective," laughingly yelled the police officer. "Don't shoot her, trooper, or we'll be under our quota. She's the only female cop we have."

Brand immediately holstered his revolver. He approached her.

"Ain't you going to apologize? Man, you scared the living hell out of me," said the detective.

"There's nothin' to apologize for. What if you hadn't been a detective and were the shooter? You could've blown me full of holes with the gun you were holding. This way, we're both alive."

"Yeah, you're right. An ambulance is on the way, but they've bought the farm." The detective tilted her head towards the two men.

Brand knelt beside the first man.

"Where were they hit?"

"Don't know on that one. The other fellow got it in the heart with a .22."

Brand directed the beam of his flashlight into the man's eyes. His pupils didn't respond. His eyelids fluttered, one not coordinated with the other. He placed his finger over the carotid artery. There was no pulse.

He walked to the second man and knelt behind him. Brand gently lifted his head and placed it in his lap. He pulled up his shirt. He saw the small entry wound in the middle of his chest. There was no blood except for the red dot the size of a pencil eraser over the entry wound. Brand felt his weak pulse stop. He died while Brand cradled his head in his hands.

"Detective."

"Yeah."

"Here's the license number of the man who directed me here. He said he saw a woman standing over two men, that she was holding a gun. Must've been you he was talking about. Anyway, here it is. How'd you get here so quickly?" asked Brand.

"Driving by when I heard the shots. Just drove up and arrested him."

"Man, that's impressive. Why'd he shoot 'em?"

"Three blocks down the street there's a homosexual bar. These two dumb sonsabitches went in and harassed the queers. The bartender got pissed, grabbed a gun, and ran after them. Caught up to 'em here. Then shot 'em. Got a wife and two kids at home, too," said the detective.

"Well, that's a strange one," said Brand.

"Most are."

"Need me for anything? If you don't, I'll get back on patrol."

"We got it."

"Okay, see ya around."

The detective nodded.

Brand walked through the gathering crowd to his patrol car. He knew this section of the city was dangerous. He loved it.

It was a laboratory full of fascinating behaviors. He thought, *Yes, Victoria, we're all animals.* He looked forward to seeing her.

"Post 93, be advised the police department has the situation under control. Resuming regular patrol."

"Do you want the name of the owner of the automobile?"

"Negative," replied Brand.

* * *

"Lieutenant, reporting as ordered, sir."

"Sit down, Bill."

"Here's a letter for you. Read it. Then we'll talk."

Dear Bill: I just want to let you know how pleased I am with the initiative you have shown in furthering your education. Your time and effort expended at the State University will certainly be rewarding to you. We, as a department, will benefit too from your experience. Please know that your request for a leave of absence is approved. You have my sincerest best wishes in this endeavor. Very truly yours, William F. Rouff, Superintendent

"You'll play basketball while you're there?" asked the lieutenant.

"No time and it'd interfere with classes. I'll be taking six classes a term plus summer school. Never liked the limelight, anyway. After the things I've seen and done as a trooper, I've learned more about life being a trooper than I could ever learn playing ball. I'm going to graduate as quickly as I can, so I can get back up here."

"Whatya mean you've learned more about life?"

Brand shrugged. "Making a mistake in basketball can result in losing a game. Making a mistake in police work can result in losing a life. Basketball's only a game, sir. People pay money to be entertained by athletes, who make lots of money for the schools and get paid nothing. Coaches call their players *kids* and not men because they never thought about the fact they're taking advantage of them. I had a professor tell me how sad it is for him to watch sports fans. They sit there in the stands, screaming and hollering for their team, and you know what, sir, the players are so focused they can't even think about them. No matter how excited the fans get, they have no say in how the game's coached. Another professor said she got gratification from watching fans because it confirmed her view of human nature.

"Someday, athletes will wake up to how they're being used. They should get at least what work-study students get paid. Both work for the university. Scholarships beef up the illusion they're getting something. A lot of them need tutors. A lot never graduate. They're called student athletes, so colleges don't have to pay them and don't have to provide them workman's compensation when they're hurt. Years from now, folks will look at twentieth-century college sports the way we look back at sweatshops." Brand finished, "Basketball's a game, sir. Police work isn't. Police work is for keeps. Police work is real life. One mistake by a police officer can be life changing for a lot of people."

"Well stated, trooper. We're going to miss ya. You've done a good job. But why in the hell do you want to go back to school? Hell, here's where the men are. College will screw up your head, make you question everything, make ya soft."

Brand didn't say what he wanted to say. He knew a college degree wouldn't make him soft—whatever soft was—and he already knew he questioned too much. He knew it wasn't good to think too much, and he hoped the more he knew the less he'd question. "Thank you for your advice, sir. I'll guard against that."

"You do that, Bill. You do that. It was real good having ya here. "One last thing," he said with a grin. "You know what those college degree titles really mean?"

Brand frowned. "Sir?"

"You already know what 'B.S.' stands for?"

"Yup." Brand knew he didn't mean Bachelor of Science degree. He meant bullshit.

"M.S. means more of the same. Ph.D. means piled higher and deeper."

The lieutenant rose from his chair and extended his hand.

Brand discreetly wiped the sweat from his hand on his trouser leg and shook the lieutenant's hand.

"Thank you, sir. The experience here's been excellent. I look forward to getting back up here."

"Okay. Now, go find the sergeant and get signed out." He opened the door for Brand.

"Yes, sir."

Brand signed in all the gear that belonged to the patrol. Trooper Lakes drove him to his apartment.

"When are you going to start school?"

"Next week, Ron. I already scheduled six courses."

"What's the rush?"

"I want to do this, but I want to get done, so I can get back up here. What's with the lieutenant?"

"What do you mean?"

"He gave me this spiel about college making me soft. Wanted me to know he's against my going back."

"Oh, you don't know then. He quit college after his freshman year."

"Really? No, I didn't know that."

"Don't let it bother you. Just figure he hasn't got a college education so that's why he's knocking it. Old defense mechanism, you know."

Ron stopped his patrol car in front of the apartment building. He turned to Brand. "Take care, Bill. Listen, come up and see me when you get a chance."

"Sure will, Ron. Planning on it."

Brand watched Ron drive away. He knew he'd miss him most of all.

He walked up the stairs to his apartment. He wondered if Reverend Williams and the lieutenant had it right, that the word "soft" to the lieutenant had the same meaning as the word "sorrow" had to Reverend Williams, that increasing knowledge increases sorrow.

*   *   *

The excitement of going back to college was tempered because of memories of Mandy. He knew he'd never be close to her again.

The price was too high. It'd be disrespectful to the memory of their daughter that should have been, but never was, to be intimate with her.

He looked forward to seeing Victoria and to her reaction the next time he saw her. He'd make sure it looked like it was an accidental meeting. He wanted to read her face and body language before she had time to rehearse the meeting. And he wondered how he would tell Loretta about his leave of absence. He decided to arrive unexpectedly.

*   *   *

"Bill, come in!" said Loretta.

He looked at her. She had on a long, blue, terry-cloth robe. Her hair was covered with small, round curls. Two bobby pins secured each curl and made a "X."

He was surprised how tightly she hugged him. He saw Catherine peeking from beside the refrigerator.

"Hi, Catherine," he said.

She jumped back.

"What's she doing?" whispered Loretta.

"Just looking at us from beside the refrigerator."

"Well, she'll just have to get used to that, won't she, Bill?" Loretta looked into his eyes.

He looked into her eyes and forced a smile. "That's why I came over this morning. We need to talk, Loretta."

"Bill, come to the kitchen and have some breakfast. What'd you like . . . eggs, pancakes, fried bread?"

"What's fried bread?"

"You mix eggs, milk, and a pinch of salt. Then drop in the bread, soak it, take it out, and fry it. You never had it? It's real good."

"Oh, yeah, I've had it before. Just forgot for a minute. Listen Loretta, anything you want to fix is fine."

"Fried bread, then?"

"Sure."

Brand wasn't interested in food.

"Let's go to the front room for our coffee. Here's the morning paper. Back in a few minutes."

He knew she'd take the pins from her hair. He thought about Victoria. He thought about the courses he'd be taking.

Ten minutes passed. Loretta's sister came for Catherine.

Loretta returned to Brand. They were alone. Her hair was neatly combed. She'd changed to a pink, shorter, more appealing robe.

"Now, how's that for timing?"

He looked at his watch.

"Few minutes, exactly."

She smiled.

She sat on the sofa and nestled close to him.

"Loretta, my leave came through. I start classes soon."

She leaned back. "When, Bill?"

"Monday morning."

"When are you moving?"

"Think I'll head out later today."

Loretta nodded.

"I'll drive down and stay with mom tonight," he said, not looking at her.

"She'd like that," said Loretta.

"Thanks for the breakfast and coffee, Loretta. I'm tired. Better get home for some sleep."

She picked up the plate and coffee mug and put them on the kitchen counter. She *discreetly* loosened the tie of her robe. She turned and walked toward him.

"Sleep here, Bill! Catherine'll be gone all day."

"Thanks for offering, Loretta, but I better go home. Can head for mom's right after I wake up."

He wished he'd thought of a better answer.

She looked at his face. He felt trapped by her stare.

"Bill, when will I get to see you again?"

"Don't know, Loretta. I just don't know. I'll be awfully busy with my studies. Registered for six courses."

He was careful to look only at her eyes.

"You mean you'll be awfully busy with Mandy, don't you!"

Her eyes had gone narrow, intense, angry.

"Loretta, it's been two months since I've seen her."

"Bill, this is goodbye. I just know it is!"

He didn't respond. He knew it was.

"Bill, sit down. I'll be right back."

Brand wondered what she was doing. His desire to be polite was fading. He felt controlled. He wanted to leave, but he couldn't bring himself to go.

She returned. "Listen, Bill, Catherine's grown attached to you, like you're almost her father. If this is goodbye to me, then it's goodbye to her. I just called my sister. She'll have her here in five minutes."

He swallowed hard. Loretta left the room. He didn't believe Catherine had grown attached to him. He felt she considered him an intruder, someone who was taking time from her mother. Certainly, he thought, he hadn't misread that.

He saw Loretta's sister drive up with Catherine. Loretta tied her robe. After speaking briefly with her, her sister drove away.

Brand was uneasy. All along, he'd believed Loretta wanted him to avoid becoming too attached to her unless he planned to marry her. He now saw it clearly. Her rule of no sex between them was a ploy she used to demonstrate her maturity. It was part of her plan to make him leave Mandy and come to her. *It's good she doesn't know it's over with Mandy.*

Loretta and Catherine entered the room, and Catherine sat on a large rocking chair, while Loretta sat on a chair away from Brand. Where they sat made a triangle. He thought of the rule of the triangle. He was at the point of it. He knew he was trapped.

"Now listen, Cathy, Bill's gonna be leaving us. He doesn't want to spend time with us anymore."

Catherine didn't know what to do, to say, or to expect. She sat on the large rocker and looked down at the floor.

"What have you to say to Cathy, Bill?"

Loretta looked at him piercingly.

"Loretta, I have absolutely nothing to say. She's too young to understand what's going on."

Catherine looked at Brand, then looked at her mother, then looked at the floor again. "Kin I go out and play, Mummy?"

Loretta's face flushed. "Go!"

Catherine jumped from the rocker and ran outside.

Brand got up and opened the door. Loretta followed. He turned and looked at her. Her nostrils flared with each breath.

"You listen to my every word, Bill Brand. If you leave now, don't you ever come back. I spent months here after my Charlie died when Cathy and I should've been home with mama and papa. I spent months planning for us to marry. You've taken so many months from my life, from Cathy's life. You took advantage of us. You, State Trooper Bill Brand, took advantage of a widow in mourning and her child!"

Brand turned and walked toward his truck.

"Don't you dare turn your back on me! Don't you dare leave me!"

As he drove away, Loretta screamed, "Do you hear me!"

While driving away, he thought about the unpredictable life he would have had if he'd married Loretta. He thought about how she controlled the relationship. None of this would've happened if he hadn't violated the Highway Patrol's *Rules and Regulations*. All along, Brand had thought the only reason for the regulation was to protect vulnerable women from troopers. Brand learned the hard way the other reason.

EPILOGUE

AFTER HIS FIRST PHILOSOPHY CLASS, Brand walked to Eaton Hall. He knew the room Vicky taught her Marriage and Family class. He stood beside her classroom's open door, waiting for her class to end.

He heard her say, "To summarize what I said today, remember I said lust is erotic, attraction is romance, and attachment is commitment. All three feelings are the result of chemicals floating around in our brains. They exist to make us want to breed so our species can survive. These hormones exist for us to have children, to continue our species, creating order in our universe, so our species can survive and evolve. At our next class, I'll talk about these and other hormones. Any questions?"

"Professor Whitcombe, does knowing these things take away the thrill of romance, the excitement of it all?" a girl asked.

"Young lady, you're asking me a personal question, and I'll answer it. For me, it's exactly the opposite. This knowledge is exactly what I need because knowing these things makes my life easier. I know I'm an animal. I know the right man for me because I know the biology of human behavior. I know the science of love."

"Who is he, Professor Whitcombe?" she asked.

"You're asking me your second personal question, young lady, and I'm invoking my constitutional right to remain silent.

"Class dismissed."

Brand quickly walked from her classroom to her office. He turned around and slowly walked back toward her classroom.

Professor Victoria Whitcombe saw Brand in the hallway.

"Bill, do you have time to walk home with me? I need to talk with you."

"Just finished my philosophy class. I have time. Let's walk."

"What'd you talk about in class, Bill?"

"Stoicism, the *Enchiridion*. It's fascinating."

"Why?"

"It's really odd, Vicky, the timing of it all. The professor asked the class if there's anything related to philosophy we wanted to ask about. No one spoke up, so I mentioned the *Enchiridion*. You should've seen his face light up! He asked me where I learned about the *Enchiridion*. I said at the Highway Patrol Academy. He's an outstanding teacher. Dr. Markus. Do you know him?"

"Yes, I know him, his wife, too. I heard he's excellent. Students love him. He retired from the Marine Corps rank of major general. You and he should get along real fine. His wife and I are friends. Some professors don't like him, though."

"Why?"

"Envy, Bill. He's got real-world experience and command presence. Male professors who don't have their act together feel insufficient and ineffectual around him."

"What about women professors . . . they like him?"

"Depends. Radical feminists hate him. Stay away from them, Bill. Trust me, they'll hate you, too."

"Why? I've never done anything to them."

"Doesn't matter. Radical feminists just don't like self-confident men."

"It's that bad, huh?"

"They're just full of hubris. In time, they'll fly too close to the sun and tumble into the sea like Icarus. I'm working on a book about cognitive dissonance."

"You got an example of cognitive dissonance?"

"The more money you lose betting on a horse, the better you think the horse is," she said.

"I think the radical feminists can't help the way they are. In fact, Vicky, I don't think any of us can help the way we are."

"You're right, Bill. That's why Professor Markus cuts them a lot of slack. He feels sorry for them."

"What about other women faculty? They like Markus?"

"Love him. His wife's bright and attractive, too, and she has all the social graces. Let's get back on topic. I took a philosophy course my freshman year. I don't remember hearing anything about the *Enchiridion*. What's it?"

"It's an ancient Greek manual of ethical advice for leaders. The *Enchiridion* teaches: Before we can manage events that happen to us, we first have to know how to manage ourselves. We must be resilient, must have a strong core, must never be quitters."

"That sounds like me. I didn't know there's a manual called the *Enchiridion*."

"My brain just can't relax, Vicky. It's always analyzing. People tell me I think too much."

"You don't think too much. You think! Most people don't. They run on emotion and mess up their lives big time. I'm home. Now I'll give you something else to think about."

He didn't want physical intimacy, didn't want her to want it. He wanted much more from her—intellectual intimacy. He wanted to talk with her, wanted to get inside her brain and have her get inside his. "What you want me to think about, Vicky?"

"Will you go with me behind the house, sit on the swing by the lake and talk?"

"Let's do that, Vicky."

*   *   *

"Bill, I must be upfront with you. I know what I feel for you, but I'm not sure what you feel for me. I know how the brain reacts to the hormones that wash over it at different stages of a relationship. But before we talk any further, I need you to know something."

"What's that, Victoria?"

"You need to know if we plan to see each other you can't enroll in any psychology course on this campus. I'm a tenured professor in the Psychology Department. People will talk if you take a psychology course from me or from anyone in our department."

"I won't be taking any psychology courses, Vicky. That's what you needed me to know?"

"Yes, that's what I needed you to know."

"Are there any skeletons in your closest, Vicky?"

"No . . . *there're plenty of books*, but no skeletons. Any skeletons in your closest?"

"None, Vicky, and there're no girlfriends."

"Children?" she asked.

"Little girl. She died. She was aborted."

Victoria said nothing.

"That everything you wanted to say to me, Vicky?"

"There's more. I'm ten years older than you. I've been waiting a long time to find the right man. Bill, you *are* the right man."

"Are you planning on marrying me?"

"I am."

"Is this a proposal, Vicky?"

"Not yet. Right now what I'm hoping for is a commitment that from this point forward you and I are in an exclusive relationship."

"From this point forward, Vicky, you and I are in an exclusive relationship. Are you planning on having children with me?"

"I am. I want us to sell this house. I want us to live in the country. I want us to have a garden, to grow flowers, to grow girls and boys, and I want us to have a yellow Labrador retriever."

Bill laughed, then leaned over, put his arm around her, kissed her cheek, and said, "Let's grow old together, Vicky. In fifty years, I will kiss you on this same cheek, and I'll say to you, 'Old woman, we've traveled a long way together.'"

She looked up into his eyes and whispered, "In fifty years I'll look into your eyes the way I'm looking into them now and say to you, 'Old man, we sure have, and I wouldn't have had it any other way.'"

RESOURCES

Brand. Henrik Ibsen. 1865.

Magnificent Obsession. A film by Douglas Sirk. 1954.

The Enchiridian by Epictetus. Written 135 A.C.E.

Ships That Pass in the Night. Beatrice Harraden. 1893.

BRAND'S "THOUGHTS FOR LIVING" LIST

People are who they are; therefore, acknowledge their reasons that give them peace of mind. If they change, it's usually on their own initiative, independent of, and often resistant to, pressure or expectations from me. (*Enchiridion*)

The art of being wise is the art of knowing what to overlook. (*Enchiridion*)

Don't do anything with the expectation of being appreciated. (*Enchiridion*)

Don't seek to have events happen as I want them to happen, but instead to happen as they do happen. (*Enchiridion*)

I'm not upset by events themselves, but by what I tell myself about those events. (*Enchiridion*)

Assume that all events happen for my own good; what benefit is hidden in this trial? (*Enchiridion*)

Be calm. Some things are up to me, and some things are not up to me. Practice calm resiliency. (*Enchiridion*)

My opponent is not the other person; it is my own thinking. (*Enchiridion*)

Other persons have freedom of speech. They can say whatever they want about me; in fact, I give them permission. (*Enchiridion*)

Think outside the box, and see the issue from another angle. (*Enchiridion*)

My master is the one with power over what I crave or fear, either to obtain or take away. To be free, I won't crave or fear anything that's up to others; otherwise, I'll be their slave. (*Enchiridion*)

We are actors in a play written by someone else. (*Enchiridion*)

Everything is transient and nothing lasts. (*Enchiridion*)

If I desire or resist things beyond my control, I'll be disappointed. (*Enchiridion*)

Watch your thoughts; they become your words. Watch your words; they become your actions. Watch your actions; they become your habits. Watch your habits; they become your character. Watch your character; it becomes your destiny. (*Lao Tzu*)

QUESTIONS AND TOPICS FOR DISCUSSION

The pre-frontal cortex is the part of the brain that controls impulsivity and decision making; it reaches its full potential when a person is in his or her mid-twenties. Discuss if Brand was too young to be a state trooper.

How has law enforcement changed since Brand's highway patrol? Are the human issues the same?

Do you think Brand will be a better man after he learned about Reverend Tanner's suicide?

Why do you think Professor Whitcombe looked unfavorably upon some male college professors and radical feminists?

Is peer pressure not to excel and to be one of the group a positive aspect of human behavior? What do you think Captain Jorden was looking for when he ordered the cadets to break ranks and run at top speed? Was it wise for Brand to increase his lead and win the race?

What did the instructors and administrative staff members want to see in the behaviors of the cadets when they boxed? Why?

Was Brand's idea of not showing weaknesses learned in the training academy, or are people who innately have this trait attracted to law enforcement? If law enforcement focuses on recruiting people who have this stoic personality trait, will they be as successful recruiting women as they are in recruiting men? What type of personalities might the women have?

Discuss if half-priced meals and free coffee are bribes. Are officers who frequent these establishments providing equal protection to other establishments that don't have this practice? Should law-enforcement agencies enforce a policy that their officers must pay the same price that all other customers are charged?

Why do police academies require their recruits to be in excellent physical shape but permit officers to become overweight and out of shape as the years pass? Should police management do something about this? If so, what should be done?

Do you believe police officers engage in more illicit sexual behavior than people do in other occupations? Why?

People who work in professions that deal with the dead eventually develop defense mechanisms that permit them to do their jobs without great emotional stress. Can humor or callousness be misinterpreted as showing lack of respect for the dead?

Police officers like catching violators. Should this not be so?

Did Brand overreact after he learned about Mandy's abortion?

Is Brand the type of man who can complement Victoria throughout a fifty-year marriage?

Is Victoria the type of woman who can complement Brand throughout a fifty-year marriage?

Many law-enforcement agencies compete with other law-enforcement agencies. Why?

Should police departments have a regulation that officers can't develop sexual relationships with people met in the line of duty? Why?

Should a university have a regulation that a professor cannot develop a sexual relationship with a student? Why?

Refute or support Professor Whitcombe's view that real-world work experience or applied research experience in the area that a professor teaches makes him or her a better teacher.

Did Brand use good judgment by making suggestions to the sheriff's major in the presence of his deputies?

Was the state patrol practice of penalty transfers reasonable? Was it fair to troopers? Was it fair to the trooper's family?

Discuss how Brand felt when he learned he was part of the scheme that trapped Trooper Jonsen.

Did Brand use good judgment in speaking at his first Post meeting? Is this an example of being well trained but not well seasoned?

Why does catching a person speeding have to be done fairly while trickery can be used when serving a warrant?

Was Brand's situation different from the other officers who followed up on a female contacted in the line of duty? Does intent make any difference?

Brand was asleep standing on his feet. He came within a fraction of a second of killing a man who had been driving under suspension. Was Brand's stoic-personality trait the reason he didn't use sick leave and reported for duty severely sleep deprived? What should Brand learn from this experience?

Why has the practice of not claiming overtime changed in most law enforcement agencies?

Discuss whether a law enforcement officer should be granted the right to be a member of a labor union. Discuss if a member of the military should be granted this right. Discuss if any local, state, or federal employee should be granted the right to be a member of a labor union.

Is there now a lower level of *esprit de corps* than what was presented in Brand's highway patrol? Was his reverence for the highway patrol healthy for him? Was it healthy for the patrol?

Give examples and support your position whether you think Brand thought too much.

Why was the bed-making demonstration the first lesson taught at the academy?

Situational awareness is knowing what's going on and what you're going to do about it. Present and discuss an incident where Brand wasn't aware he'd lost situational awareness.

What is the best statement from Brand's "Thoughts for Living" list that applies to each chapter and to the Epilogue? Why?

CPSIA information can be obtained
at www.ICGtesting.com
Printed in the USA
LVHW012250210822
726491LV00009B/486